THE ETHICS
OF HUMAN
CLONING

Other Books in the At Issue Series:

THE ETHICS
OF HUMAN
CLONING

William Dudley, *Book Editor*

David L. Bender, *Publisher*
Bruno Leone, *Executive Editor*

Bonnie Szumski, *Editorial Director*
Stuart B. Miller, *Managing Editor*

An Opposing Viewpoints® Series

Greenhaven Press, Inc.
San Diego, California

Library of Congress Cataloging-in-Publication Data

The Ethics of human cloning / William Dudley, editor.
        p.   cm. — (At issue)
    Includes bibliographical references and index.
    ISBN 0-7377-0471-3 (pbk. : alk. paper) —
ISBN 0-7377-0472-1 (lib. bdg. : alk. paper)
    1. Human cloning—Moral and ethical aspects. I. Dudley,
William, 1964– . II. Series: At issue (San Diego, Calif.)

QH442.2 .E847 2001
174'.25—dc21   00-046229
                                                                    CIP

© 2001 by Greenhaven Press, Inc., PO Box 289009,
San Diego, CA 92198-9009

Printed in the U.S.A.

Table of Contents

Introduction

To clone a living thing is to make an exact genetic copy of that organism. Individual genes—the biochemical building blocks that govern the structure and function of all living creatures—can be cloned, as can whole cells. Both gene and cell cloning are common research tools in current genetic and biomedical research.

Entire organisms can also be cloned. For example, humans have cloned plants for centuries by use of small cuttings—a process called vegetative propagation. Some invertebrate animals—starfish and earthworms, for example,—grow into two identical organisms when split apart, but most animals differ from plants in that they cannot be cloned so readily.

In the 1980s scientists began researching methods of cloning higher-order animals—mammals in particular. The accelerating success of their experiments has led to widespread discussion over the possibility of human cloning. This discussion has revealed widespread disagreement, both within the scientific community and the general public, over whether human cloning research should be allowed.

Two types of cloning

There are two general methods of cloning in higher animals, and both have been the subject of scientific study. One already occurs naturally for some humans when identical twins or triplets are born. This happens when the fertilized egg (a zygote), early in the process of development, divides into two separate parts, each of which develops into a genetically identical individual. In the 1980s this same process was artificially stimulated in cattle. The first experiments in artificially stimulating twinning in humans were done in 1993 by researchers in George Washington University in Washington, D.C. (The researchers deliberately performed their cloning experiments on genetically abnormal embryos that had no chance of survival.)

The other method of cloning is called nuclear transplantation. In this procedure, the nucleus of a cell (where virtually all the genetic material is located) is transplanted into or fused with an egg whose nucleus has been removed. When most people talk about the prospect of human cloning, they envision the use of some kind of nuclear transplantation. This is something that, as of September 2000, has yet to be done in humans, and is not even known to have been attempted.

For many years, most scientists have maintained that using nuclear transplantation to create a clone from a mature cell of a mammal was impossible because of formidable biological barriers. While all mammalian cells contain the same full genetic information as the original fertilized egg, they have become specialized. As cells develop some genetic instructions are turned off and others turned on so that some cells become skin cells, others form nerves, still others form blood cells, and so on. What scientists could not figure out was how to take, for example, a skin cell and reprogram it to not create more skin cells, but instead to subdivide into different cells and develop into a whole new animal. In the 1980s and 1990s scientists successfully cloned mammals via nuclear transplantation, but these experiments used cell nuclei from developing embryos, not from adult animals.

Then, in early 1997, researchers in Scotland stunned the world by announcing that they had successfully used nuclear transplantation to create a clone of an adult sheep. In a sense, the clone, named "Dolly," had three female parents: The nucleus of an udder cell from one sheep was fused with an enucleated egg cell from a second sheep and the resulting embryo was then placed in the uterus of a third. Dolly became a celebrity of sorts, and later became a mother (through ordinary reproductive methods), demonstrating that she was a fully functioning adult.

The scientists who created Dolly disavowed any intention of cloning humans, saying the purpose of their research was to perfect methods of mass-producing genetically identical animals. However, the announcement caused much public furor centered on the prospect of cloning human beings. A *Time*/CNN poll found 93 percent of Americans expressing disapproval of human cloning. Many bioethicists and scientists spoke out against human cloning. The Roman Catholic Church called for a universal ban on human cloning, while President Bill Clinton announced a moratorium on federal funding of cloning research.

In response to public concern, the National Bioethics Advisory Commission (NBAC), an expert panel created by Clinton to explore ethical issues surrounding the biotechnology industry, was given the task of investigating the issue. After taking testimony from scientists, ethicists, religious leaders, and others, NBAC recommended in June 1997 a three-to-five-year continuation of the previously announced moratorium on cloning research designed to create a human child. Research on cloning of human cells and tissues, the NBAC said, should be continued.

Ethical questions

The ethical questions people have raised about human cloning exist on several levels. Some objections concern the safety of human cloning experiments. Cloning is far from being an infallible process. It took 277 attempts to create Dolly—the other fused egg cells failed to develop or had abnormalities that proved fatal during gestation. The prospect of a similar failure/success ratio involving humans is grounds enough to ban cloning research, some argue. In addition, questions linger as to the long-term physical health and possible premature aging of clones such as Dolly the sheep. NBAC concluded in its June 1997 report that such safety questions warranted a moratorium on human cloning reproduction experiments.

The safety and premature aging concerns surrounding cloning are technical barriers that may or may not fall as the science of cloning advances. However, many people have raised ethical objections to cloning that go beyond questions of safety. For some, cloning violates fundamental religious beliefs on how human reproduction should occur. Others worry that cloning could blur traditional family relationships. A clone could be seen as both a person's daughter and twin sister, for instance.

Other ethical questions focus on motives for human cloning and whether some reasons are more acceptable than others. For instance, people might deem it ethical for a couple at risk of bearing children with a genetic disorder to clone one of the clearly healthy parents. But would it be ethical for a couple to clone a child simply because the father desired a genetic replica of himself? Would it be ethical for parents to take cells from a child who had died suddenly in an accident and clone a "replacement," since that second child could be subject to unfair expectations? Moreover, some people question whether society has any right to intrude on the reproductive decisions of couples and individuals by imposing any restrictions on cloning.

A principle that forms the basis for many human cloning arguments is the assertion by the German philosopher Immanuel Kant that humans must be treated as *ends* in themselves, not as *means* to an end. Perhaps the starkest application of such reasoning is the possibility that humans might be cloned in order to provide organs that could be transplanted into the genetic donor without fear of rejection. The use of cloned embryos and fetuses for such purposes is defended by some cloning advocates and dismissed by others as a far-fetched scenario that would never really happen. But many would agree that creating a clone of a person simply as a source of "spare parts" is a gross violation of Kant's principle.

Some people go further and argue that cloning for any purpose violates Kant's principle on some level because a "manufactured" clone would be burdened by specific expectations on what kind of person he or she would become. "There is a profound ethical difference," argued the late Catholic archbishop John O'Connor, "between 'having a child' and 'making a child.' A child begotten can always be seen as a gift, whereas a child made or manufactured can always be seen as a thing—a product for use not to be respected for what he/she is, but priced for what it can do." But others reject the argument that just because a person is a clone, he or she would not be treated and loved as any other human would be. "Why suppose that cloned persons wouldn't share the same rights and dignity as the rest of us?" asks bioethics professor Ruth Macklin.

Supporters of human cloning argue that the initial negative reaction is simply a common human response to something new and unknown, and compare cloning to other assisted reproductive techniques such as in vitro fertilization. When the idea of taking a woman's egg out of the body, fertilizing it in the laboratory, and implanting it back in the womb was first attempted in the 1970s, many people found the procedure disturbing and unnatural, and wondered how "test-tube" babies would fare socially and psychologically. But today in vitro fertilization is accepted by most people as an acceptable way for infertile couples to have their own children. Cloning advocates argue that attitudes toward cloning will undergo a similar evolution and the procedure will come to be seen as an acceptable alternative for infertile people who want to have children.

Whether or not human cloning will eventually be as common—and accepted—as in vitro fertilization remains to be seen, but it is clear that the ethical debate over human cloning will not soon die down. The authors of *At Issue: The Ethics of Human Cloning* present a variety of perspectives on the issues raised by the as yet unrealized prospect of human cloning.

1

Ethical Issues of Human Cloning: An Overview

Michael Woods

Michael Woods is science editor of the Pittsburgh Post-Gazette.

The announcement in 1997 of the successful cloning of an adult sheep led to widespread concern that human beings might be next to be cloned. Polls indicated that the majority of Americans thought that cloning of humans was immoral, while church officials, political leaders, and ethicists generally reacted negatively to the idea of human cloning (even if they supported the cloning of animals). Supporters of cloning research argued that much of the public's concern was based on misconceptions about what exactly cloning is and how it works. While no one has yet attempted human cloning, it poses a future challenge as society weighs its potential costs and benefits.

S cientists in Scotland shocked the world on February 22, 1997, by announcing that they had *cloned* (produced an exact genetic copy of) an adult sheep. The resulting ewe, born in July 1996 and named Dolly, represented a major advance in genetics research. She was the first clone of an adult mammal. Later in 1997, scientists announced that they had used various cloning techniques to produce other sheep (capable of secreting proteins potentially useful in pharmaceuticals) as well as monkeys and calves. By the end of 1997, it seemed to many observers that cloning technology was on the verge of revolutionizing livestock breeding, drug production, and medical research.

Immediately after the announcement of Dolly's birth, however, church officials, theologians, ethicists, and politicians voiced the widespread concern that human beings might be cloned, and this ignited an international ethical and legal debate. While scientists claimed they had no intention of cloning humans, the creation of Dolly proved that it was technically possible to take a body cell from a human being and use it to clone that person. People recalled such science-fiction tales as the 1978 movie *The Boys from Brazil,* in which Nazis living in South America cloned Adolf Hitler from preserved tissue, and believed that a nightmare was about to come true. What if an individual with the means to do so decided to produce dozens of copies of himself or herself? What if parents desired a "designer child"—a clone, perhaps, of supermodel Cindy Crawford, basketball star Michael Jordan, or chess champion Garry Kasparov? What if parents stopped giving birth to babies and, instead, reproduced themselves from skin cells? Would human cloning lead to people produced solely to serve as donors for organ transplants? Would babies that were products of cloning grow up to be normal, or would they be defective in some way?

Reaction to Dolly

Polls taken in February 1997 revealed the public's concern. A Gallup Poll indicated that 88 percent of people in the United States thought that the cloning of a human being would be "morally wrong," and a TIME/CNN poll indicated that 74 percent of Americans thought that human cloning was "against God's will." Among the religious organizations that spoke out against human cloning was the Roman Catholic Church, which, four days after Dolly's announcement, called for a global ban on human cloning.

Politicians generally reacted negatively to the news of Dolly's birth. In March 1997, the British government announced that it planned to stop providing funds for cloning research at the Scottish institute where Dolly was produced. Also in March, U.S. President Bill Clinton warned scientists against the temptation "to play God," and he issued a 90-day moratorium on the use of U.S. government funds for research into the cloning of humans. Clinton also asked the National Bioethics Advisory Commission (NBAC)—a panel of 18 experts in science, law, and ethics— to develop recommendations for a national policy on human cloning. (The NBAC had been created by Clinton in 1995 to explore the ethical issues concerning the biotechnology industry.) The U.S. Congress introduced two bills that, if passed, would permanently ban federal funding for research into human cloning. A third bill would mandate a $5,000 fine on anyone conducting such research. Senator Christopher Bond of Missouri, the sponsor of one of the bills, said, "There are aspects of human life that should be off limits to science."

---

74 percent of Americans thought that human cloning was "against God's will."

The Public Health and Safety Subcommittee of the Senate Labor and Human Resources Committee held a hearing in March 1997 during which several scientists and ethicists presented their opinions on cloning. Among those testifying before the subcommittee was Ian Wilmut, the scientist who led the team that produced Dolly. Wilmut surprised many when he announced that he too supported a ban on human cloning. He said that he had never heard of an ethically acceptable reason for cloning a human. When Senator Tom Harkin of Iowa predicted human cloning in his lifetime, Wilmut replied, "I hope you're wrong."

What is a clone?

As the controversy raged, it became apparent that public leaders were often confused as to what a clone is and is not. A clone is an exact genetic copy of a gene, a cell, or a whole organism (such as a plant or animal). The clone contains precisely the same genetic information as the original. The cells of a tumor, for example, originate from a single cancer cell and are, therefore, clones. Identical twins originate from division of a fertilized egg into two identical eggs. They are clones. Copies of genes or cells made through genetic engineering are also clones. When applied to whole plants or animals, cloning means producing an identical individual *asexually* (without fusion of an egg and sperm).

Plant breeders have long employed cloning techniques to produce desired varieties of plants without use of seeds. Most apple trees, for example, are grown from buds cut from trees that have previously produced a desired kind of fruit. The buds are *grafted* (attached by placing into slits cut in plants) to roots of other trees. The resulting apple trees are clones of the trees from which the buds were cut.

In the 1950's, scientists developed a technique called nuclear transfer to produce clones of certain kinds of animals. In nuclear transfer, scientists remove the *nucleus* (the part of a cell that contains an organism's genetic information and controls growth and development) from an unfertilized egg cell and replace it with the nucleus of a cell—called the donor cell—taken from another organism. The resulting cell develops into a small embryo, which is implanted into the womb of a surrogate mother. Following the pregnancy, the surrogate mother gives birth to an offspring genetically identical to the organism from which the donor cell was taken. This technique, originally used to clone frogs, was first applied to the cloning of mammals in the 1980's—using donor cells taken from mouse embryos.

Making of Dolly

Dolly was produced with a new variation of nuclear transfer developed by Wilmut, Keith H.S. Campbell, and their colleagues at the Roslin Institute and PPL Therapeutics PLC, both near Edinburgh, Scotland. The birth of Dolly shocked scientists because she was produced from a donor cell taken from an adult rather than from an embryo. Many researchers had previously tried to transfer nuclei from cells taken from adults, but the resulting embryos had died. These failures led scientists to conclude that only the genes of an embryo had the ability to direct the development of a complete individual. They also assumed that genes lose this ability as their cells become part of specialized tissue, such as skin, muscle, nerve, bone, and hair. Cloning an adult mammal appeared to be impossible.

The researchers in Scotland accomplished the seemingly impossible by removing cells from the udder of a 6-year-old ewe and depriving them of almost all nutrients for five days. Wilmut and Campbell believed that nutrient deprivation would help to reprogram genes in the cells, making them capable of directing the development of a complete animal. To produce Dolly, the scientists fused one of the reprogrammed udder cells with an *enucleated* (without a nucleus) egg cell from another ewe. The resulting embryo was placed in a surrogate mother ewe, which gave birth to Dolly 148 days later. The technique employed by Wilmut and his colleagues was inefficient in that it was repeated 277 times before yielding a surviving offspring. In August 1997, a U.S. company announced that it had developed a more efficient and advanced cloning technique that enabled them, within only 15 attempts, to produce a calf.

As the controversy raged, it became apparent that public leaders were often confused as to what a clone is and is not.

The reason scientists first cloned mammals from adult cells was to develop a better way of producing *transgenic* animals (animals with genes from species other than their own) for commercial and medical use. The biotechnology firm that helped fund research on Dolly, PPL Therapeutics, genetically alters female mammals to produce human proteins in their milk and investigates how such proteins could be used to treat human diseases. The first such transgenic animal produced through cloning, a sheep named Polly, was introduced to the press in July 1997 by the same scientists who created Dolly. Besides being used to produce pharmaceutically useful proteins, transgenic animals can be used to improve livestock and to produce modified organs capable of being transplanted into humans. The techniques currently employed to produce transgenic animals are expensive, slow, and inefficient. Experts hoped that cloning might streamline the production of such animals—enabling them to be mass produced.

Concerns about human cloning

While many scientists and medical ethicists applaud the cloning of research animals, a number of them nevertheless fear the consequences of any attempts to clone humans. In early June 1997, NBAC concluded that cloning was not yet safe enough for use with humans, because attempts at human cloning could result in the loss of many embryos and fetuses. Also, no one knows what the long-term health effects of cloning might be. Any attempt to create a child through cloning, therefore, would be "morally unacceptable." The panel noted that cloning research should be allowed to continue as long as the researchers do not try to use human embryos to create babies. NBAC recommended that President Clinton's moratorium on the use of federal funds for human cloning research be continued indefinitely and that Congress consider passing a law making it illegal to create a child through cloning. The panel recommended that such a law should expire in three to five years, allowing Congress to review advances in cloning technology and determine whether a continued ban was justified. President Clinton sent a bill to Congress that embodied the panel's recommendations.

In apparent justification of NBAC's cautionary recommendations, scientists said in late June that some of Dolly's *chromosomes* (structures that carry genes) had undergone subtle changes normally found only in cells from older animals. These changes, which probably resulted from the fact that the cell used to produce Dolly came from a 6-year-old ewe, raised the possibility that Dolly could age and die prematurely. Dolly also might face a high risk of genetic defects because her genes were inherited only from a female animal. An organism may need a complete set of maternal and paternal genes. Scientific evidence indicates that some genes work normally only when inherited from the father, and others work normally only when inherited from the mother.

Possible psychological effects?

The ethical debate over cloning also encompassed the possible psychological impact on the offspring. Would a human clone tend to have a diminished sense of individuality? Perhaps human clones would think that they were genetically destined to the same fate as the persons from whom their donor cells came.

Ethical questions have also been raised about cloning's effects on parenting and family life. Parents of clones might value their children according to how closely they met some overly detailed, preordained specifications. Cloning, therefore, could undermine basic elements of a loving, nurturing family, such as the acceptance of each child as a unique individual.

Cloning might have society-wide effects, as well. What would happen to a world that separated reproduction from love and other human relationships? Would society use cloning for *eugenics* (attempting to scientifically improve the human race according to arbitrary standards)? Ethicists have voiced concerns that cloning, combined with various techniques of genetic engineering, could lead to efforts to selectively breed children who are healthier, more intelligent, or even designed for warfare or slavery.

Misconceptions about cloning

Scientists and medical ethicists who argue in favor of human cloning claim that much of the public's concern is based on misconceptions. They note that, although many people believe that cloning would produce an instant carbon copy of an adult person, cloning would, in reality, produce what amounts to a delayed identical twin, several years or even decades younger than the person who donated the cell from which the clone was produced. Identical twins are genetic carbon copies, but they are separate individuals. They often look different because of different preferences in clothing and hairstyle. They may have different moral values, academic achievements, occupations, and tastes in music.

Another misconception that scientists suggest clouds the issue of human cloning is the question of how genes influence an individual's development. Human beings do not inherit a fixed, unchangeable genetic blueprint from their parents. Scientists believe that physical and mental traits result from complex interactions between genes and the environment in which an individual grows up and lives—including the chemical environment surrounding the fetus in the womb. Two people can inherit the same set of genes and turn out very differently, because environmental factors often determine how genes are expressed. A person might, for example, inherit genes for large body size, but those genes will not be fully expressed unless the person receives proper nutrition. Genes for musical ability may be expressed only if a person grows up in a family that loves music.

While many scientists and medical ethicists applaud the cloning of research animals, a number of them nevertheless fear the consequences of any attempts to clone humans.

Some ethicists voice fears that human clones might be considered less than human and might be used for spare parts in organ transplants or for other unethical purposes. Legal experts, however, claim that clones would have all the legal rights and protections of other people. They note that society never questioned the legal rights of offspring resulting from other reproductive technologies, such as *in vitro fertilization* (the technology that produces "test-tube babies").

Perhaps the strongest argument put forth in favor of human cloning is that cloning could provide the only avenue available to some infertile couples for producing children. In cases of fertile couples in which one member carries a gene for a disease, cloning using a cell from the other member could assure that the couple has a healthy child of its own. Some U.S. legal experts claim that preventing a couple from choosing cloning as a method of reproduction could be unconstitutional. Scientists and ethicists who favor human cloning research also argue that cloning may provide a better understanding of the nature of genetic diseases and aid in the production of embryos from which cells could be obtained to grow various organs for organ transplants.

Will humans be cloned?

Although many laboratories around the world conducted animal cloning research in 1997, no laboratory acknowledged that it attempted to clone humans. However, noting that when a feat is technically possible, it is usually performed, a number of ethicists stated that it was simply a matter of time before a human being would be cloned. They argued that governments should establish strict regulations based on conditions under which human cloning might be acceptable, rather than spend time creating unenforceable laws that ban the procedure.

To much of the public, the sudden possibility of human cloning might have seemed like the latest in a series of radical and frightening scientific developments that society has had to confront throughout the last century—from the splitting of the atom to the proliferation of computers, from artificial life-support systems to test-tube babies. As society at the dawn of the next century weighs the benefits versus the harm of many scientific developments, human cloning may present the most thought-provoking challenge yet.

2

The News Media and the Human Cloning Debate

Patrick D. Hopkins

Patrick D. Hopkins teaches philosophy, bioethics, and science and technology studies at the University of Colorado.

The media coverage of cloning following the announcement of the successful cloning of a sheep (Dolly) in Scotland in 1997 both revealed and created public worries about human cloning. Ethical worries about cloning centered around three central concerns: the loss of human individuality, the motivations of would-be cloners, and the fear of out-of-control scientists. Media reports on cloning also reflected two widely held ideas: that genes determine one's destiny, and that copies are inferior to the original.

Without having read a single article, heard a single presentation, or taken a single bioethics class, most Americans have already received training in the ethics of cloning. When the news that scientists had cloned an adult animal hit the airwaves and fiber optic cables of the United States, the public heard for the first time (in a venue other than the movies) that cloning an adult human was possible. But the media stories about cloning were not merely about the procedure. In fact, they were not even predominantly about the procedure. Given more time, teasing, and talk was the story about the morality of cloning. Morality was the real news, and just as the majority of people, including policymakers, got their information on the science and technology of cloning from television and print, they got their information on the ethics of cloning from those same sources. The media instructed us on the major ethical concerns of cloning, its social, religious, and psychological significance, and the motivations behind it. Media coverage fixed the content and outline of the public moral debate, both revealing and creating the dominant public worries about the possibility of cloning humans. It is important then to examine the ethical story the media has told, for being cast much

Reprinted from "Bad Copies: How Popular Media Represent Cloning as an Ethical Problem," by Patrick D. Hopkins, *Hastings Center Report*, March/April 1998. Copyright © 1998 by the Hastings Center. Reprinted by permission.

more broadly than academic bioethics debates, it will more widely affect social policy and general attitudes.

Although there are, of course, diverse messages sent through the media, in my investigation of television, magazine, newspaper, and online reports, the primary characterization of cloning as an ethical issue centers around three connected worries: the loss of human uniqueness and individuality, the pathological motivations of anyone who would want to clone, and the fear of "out-of-control" science creating a "brave new world."[1]

Copies and losing uniqueness

While many traditional ethical concerns might be generated by cloning—worries about medical risk, the use and loss of embryos, cost and availability, using humans as means—overwhelmingly the media focused on the supposed danger to individuality and uniqueness. This paramount concern about losing our uniqueness (and even our identities) results from anxiety over the status of clones as copies. It is impossible to demonstrate the extent to which the media has fixated on the fear of copies without actually showing the many images and playing the many sound bites, but perhaps at least a sense of this fixation can be conveyed through the following examples:

• A *Time* magazine cover shows an image of the Sistine Chapel, but now there are five identical Adam's hands and the question "Where do we draw the line?" The contents page shows an infant's photograph, multiplied by twelve, and the question, "Is this a promising technique or a path to madness?" The spread accompanying the main story shows what appears to be an average middle-class couple with their children, except they have eight identical sons (8 November 1993).

• Another *Time* cover shows two large identical pictures of sheep on a background of thirty or more smaller copies of the same picture, asking "Will There Ever Be Another You?" The contents page announces the creation of a "carboncopy." The photo spread introducing the main story shows a coinoperated gumball machine dispensing identical white males by the dozen. A later picture shows identical human bodies dropping out of a test tube (10 March 1997).

• A *Newsweek* cover sports three identical babies in lab beakers. Inside is a picture of Warhol's "The Twenty Marilyns" (10 March 1997).

• *U.S. News & World Report* features a drawing of an ink stamp pressing out copies of babies. An enlargement of the same picture shows one of the baby-copies crying—intimating unhappiness with either being a clone or being cloned (10 March 1997).

• ABC's *Nightline* program opens with this tease: "What if you could make an exact copy of a human being? What if you could make as many as you wanted? You could make a copy of a deceased relative. Or a copy of yourself—your perfect organ donor." Then a picture of an angelic baby is multiplied over and over until there are scores of identical infants.

Genetic determinism

This representation of cloning as a frightening mass production of sameness reflects two powerful and widespread ideas. The first is a belief in genetic determinism. Ordinarily, the common public response on news and talk shows to claims about the genetic determination of violent behavior, or adultery, or even happiness is skepticism or rejection. The reason seems to be a reluctance to allow anyone to "get away" with proscribed behavior or to believe that one's own happiness or success is predetermined. It is somewhat odd, then, that the reports on cloning indicate a public belief that a clone will be psychologically identical to his or her donor. As it turns out, however, the media reports contain little evidence that the U.S. public does in fact suddenly believe in genetic determinism. The reports simply assume that it does and then attempt to disabuse the public of its error. But most television and magazine stories engage in a confusing, contradictory bit of double-talk (or double-show). The images and not-very-clever headlines all convey unsettling messages that clones will be exact copies, while inside the stories go to some effort to educate us that clones will not in fact be exact copies.

On the *Nightline* program, which first teased viewers with replicating babies, the reporter asks what it means that scientists could create a genetic copy of him. He says:

> If I expect that baby to become another me, a copy, no way, because he can't live my life, can't have my accidents, my good luck, my bad luck, my experiences. So like all identical twins who start out genetically the same, in spite of the similarities, over time they become very distinct, very different people. Environment counts. It shapes the genes, it changes them and creates difference. Says Dr. Francis Collins, head of the government's big project on human genes, "genes can't reproduce an exact copy of a person."

Scenes from the movie *The Boys from Brazil* follow this explanation, and then the summary: "So, no matter what you see in the movies, there's no way my clone could ever be an exact or even a close copy of me. Cloning will never make anybody immortal."

While many traditional ethical concerns might be generated by cloning, . . . overwhelmingly the media focused on the supposed danger to individuality and uniqueness.

On *The Charlie Rose Show,* Rose discusses the possibility of an infertile couple who want to clone themselves. One guest points out that the child would not be a copy of the parent because that child wouldn't have mom's or dad's experiences. Discussing parents who might want to clone a dying child, another guest argues that much of the ethical debate depends on fundamental misconceptions about what genes actually determine. He says that having a genetic copy might tell you something about the risk of disease, but it will tell you little about what that person will be like as an adult. Thus, these hypothetical parents who want to clone a dying child in order not to lose the child will still in fact lose the child. On the PBS *Newshour,* two interviewees both point out that it is a major mistake to think that a clone would be an exact copy. A later broadcast reiterates that the biggest popular misconception about cloning is that one would get an adult copy of oneself.

Some stories, however, are a bit more confused and ambiguous about their rejection of genetic determinism. In *Time,* Charles Krauthammer writes: "(W)hat Dolly . . . promises is not quite a second chance at life (you don't reproduce yourself; you just reproduce a twin) but another soul's chance at *your* life. . . . Here is the opportunity to pour all the accumulated learning of your life back into a new you, to raise your exact biological double, to guide your very flesh through a second existence" (10 March 1997, p. 61). But most are very clear in their texts (even while contradicting their stories with images). *Newsweek* says: "(O)n the more profound question of what, exactly, a human clone would be, doubters and believers are unanimous. A human clone might resemble, superficially, the individual from whom it was made. But it would differ dramatically in the traits that define an individual" (p. 55). *U.S. News & World Report* says: "Would a cloned human be identical to the original? Identical genes don't produce identical people. . . . Parents could clone a second child who eerily resembled their first in appearance, but all the evidence suggests the two would have very different personalities" (p. 60).

While it is admirable that most reports on cloning try to explain a little basic genetics and try to clarify some of the misconceptions about genetic determinism, it is interesting that most of the comments on determinism are geared toward allaying fears that clones will in fact be exact copies. The push in these remarks is less toward basic genetics education and more toward convincing the public that individual uniqueness is not endangered by cloning.

Is a copy inferior to the original?

This concern points to the second prominent idea at work in all those eye-catching pictures and headlines representing cloning as mass photocopying: that a copy of something is necessarily inferior to the "original" (a term of positive value itself) and that copies often devalue their "originals." Though no one quoted in the cloning reports gave any reason or argument why this would be the case, it is clear from the way copies are characterized that they are metaphysically suspect.

For example, *Time* claims: "Dolly does not merely take after her biological mother. She is a carbon copy, a laboratory counterfeit so exact that she is in essence her mother's identical twin" (10 March 1997, p. 62). The term "counterfeit" here implies that clones as copies are fakes, not as real or legitimate as the original—at least if made by humans. And the anticopy rhetoric gets more passionate. The same issue quotes Jeremy Rifkin saying: "It's a horrendous crime to make a Xerox of someone. . . . You're putting a human into a genetic straightjacket" (p. 70). A picture of one of Rifkin's protests in an earlier issue shows people holding signs that say, "I like just one of me" (8 November 1993, p. 69). The existence of human copies is not only interpreted as an assault on individuality, however, but on the very essence of human dignity. A *Time* report on embryo cloning says: "For many, the basic sanctity of life seemed to be under attack." The same issue quotes Germain Grisez, a professor of Christian ethics: "The people doing this ought to contemplate splitting themselves in half and see how they like it" (8 November 1993, p. 69). On *Nightline,* an interviewee asked about the technology behind cloning says:

> There are certain clear points, though, and one is that we have to use our technology to undergird and to build on human dignity, and human dignity, the dignity of the individual has to be at the center of this discussion and plainly the very idea of cloning introduces a problematic into the notion of human dignity. I mean, this is taking somebody's identity and giving it, at the genetic level, to somebody else. I mean, this is what it's all about. . . . Once you start doing it to people, human dignity is in the balance.

U.S. News & World Report informs us that many ethicists believe that the interest in cloning will die away, because: "Making copies, they say, pales next to the wonder of creating a unique human being the old-fashioned way" (10 March 1997, p. 59). This idea implies that clones will lack this highly desired property of uniqueness. These amorphous fears about the existence of genetic copies eating away at human dignity, uniqueness, and individuality even begin to get translated into a right of genetic uniqueness. *Time* quotes Daniel Callahan saying: "I think we have a right to our own individual genetic identity. . . . I think this could well violate that right" (8 November 1993, p. 68). In a speech replayed on PBS's *Newshour,* President Bill Clinton raises the worry about uniqueness and copying to an even grander scale: "My own view is that human cloning would have to raise deep concerns given our most cherished concepts of faith and humanity. Each human life is unique, born of a miracle that reaches beyond laboratory science. I believe we must respect this profound gift and resist the temptation to replicate ourselves."

At one and the same time, then, the media showcases, exaggerates, and mitigates concerns that clones will be dignity-damaging, individuality-damaging copies. What none of the reports does, however, is question the assumption that even exact copies would in fact have these deleterious metaphysical, moral, and social consequences for the "original" people who were cloned. Instead, even while defusing *The Boys from Brazil* scenarios, the media shores up a peculiar obsession with uniqueness—pouring the weight of that concept into genetic patterns. The belief promulgated almost seems to be that human value or human dignity is a fixed unity attached to a genetic pattern, a zerosum game in which copies of the pattern have to divide that value up among themselves. The moral and rhetorical weight attached to this idea is amazing, so much so that even the president characterizes cloning as a sinful "temptation" to "replicate ourselves."

American individualism

One has to wonder if the dominant media message about cloning is not a manifestation of a peculiar American emphasis on individualism. It is assumed that uniqueness is an unquestionable good, a paramount metaphysical virtue (an idea I would expect at least a few twins and triplets to challenge). But no one defends why being unique is better than being one of many. It is easy to imagine, however, the media in another culture with different values never mentioning the worry about copies and the loss of uniqueness. Another culture's magazines might instead focus entirely on medical risk (a topic virtually ignored in U.S. popular coverage). As it is, however, American culture's selective passion for uniqueness is threatened by the realization that humans can be copied biologically. This leads to a vaguely valuative fear that cloning is simply un-American. As *Time* puts it:

> What does the sudden ability to make genetic stencils of ourselves say about the concept of individuality? Do the ants and bees and Maoist Chinese have it right? Is a species simply an uberorganism, a collection of multicellular parts to be die-cast as needed? Or is there something about the individual that is lost when the mystical act of conceiving a person becomes standardized into a mere act of photocopying one? (10 March 1997: 67)

Cloning, *Time* worries, is on the side of robotic insects and communist ideology. Not cloning is on the side of American individualism and Mystery.

As with so many other cases, these ideological alignments lead policymakers to use the law to "protect" us and our conventional understanding of ourselves from the unromantic analyses of science. Announcing a federal moratorium on cloning humans, President Clinton said:

> What the legislation will do is to reaffirm our most cherished belief about the miracle of human life and the God-given individuality each person possesses. It will ensure that we do not fall prey to the temptation to replicate ourselves at the expense of those beliefs. . . . Banning human cloning reflects our humanity. It is the right thing to do. Creating a child through this new method calls into question our most fundamental beliefs. (*Newshour*)

It is telling that the primary reason for opposing cloning, in both the media and in the words of the chief-of-state, is that copying ourselves challenges our *beliefs* about individuality.

Motivations behind cloning

If the dominant ethical issue in cloning coverage was the metaphysical danger posed by copies, it is not surprising that people who desire cloning—who by definition want to copy themselves or others—are considered corrupt or misguided. Of course, there are extraordinarily few people in the world who currently intend to use cloning. After all, the possibility presented itself only recently, and even then it was made clear that human cloning was still a way off. However, in trying to imagine what kind of market cloning might have, the media have repeatedly discussed hypothetical scenarios. One can hardly blame people for trying to think of what uses human cloning might be put to. However, the repeated broadcast and printing of various hypothetical situations has a tremendous influence on how cloning is received—especially when these hypotheticals are laced with moral judgments. Empirically accurate or not, these hypothetical examples travel memetically through the public consciousness, becoming almost paradigmatic.[2] Even before anyone actually requests cloning, we already have a picture of the kind of people who would want it—and it's not flattering. Virtuous motives and human cloning are seen as incompatible. Here are some of the major media examples, in order of their frequency.

Virtuous motives and human cloning are seen as incompatible.

The Megalomaniac. This character is drawn from movies, whose clips were shown constantly in the days following the cloning announcement. Scenes from *The Boys from Brazil* flashed onto television screens, showing a plot to clone little Hitlers. Scenes from Woody Allen's *Sleeper,* featuring an attempt to clone an evil leader from his left-over nose, and shots of innocent people fleeing the bloodthirsty T-rex clones of *Jurassic Park* had their time as well. But fiction is frighteningly close to reality, we are told. *Nightline* instructs us that irrespective of the law, some real live fellow with enough money could clone himself if he wanted. *Time* hypothesizes a rich industrialist who has never wanted children but now "with a little help from the cloning lab . . . has the opportunity to have a son who would bear not just his name . . . but every scrap of genetic coding that makes him what he is. Now that appeals to the local industrialist. In fact, if this first boy works out, he might even make a few more" (10 March 1997, p. 70). *Time*'s assessment of this situation: "Of all the reasons for using the new technology, pure ego raises the most hackles. It's one thing to want to be remembered after you are gone; it's quite another to manufacture a living monument to ensure that you are. Some observers claim to be shocked that anyone would contemplate such a thing. But that's naïve . . ." (10 March 1997, p. 70). The same issue of *Time* warns of "the ultimate nightmare scenario," which begins: "The Despot will not be coming to the cloning lab today. Before long, he knows, the lab's science will come to him . . . (he) has ruled his little country for 30 years, but now he's getting old. . . . As soon as the technology of the cloning lab goes global—as it inevitably must—his people can be assured of his leadership long after he's gone" (p. 71). *U.S. News & World Report* also blithely informs us, in spite of previously rejecting genetic determinism, that a megalomaniac could decide to achieve immortality by cloning an "heir" (p. 60). Less objectionable but still egomaniacal examples are scattered around—brilliant scientists, great physicians, and famous athletes figure prominently as people who would love to copy themselves, or whom others would love to copy.

The Replacement Child. Usually contrasted to the megalomaniac or egomaniac as a more sympathetic middle-class motivation for cloning is the couple who hopes to "replace" a dying child. Even though *Nightline* host Chris Wallace calls this the "best-case scenario," a guest describes the situation as psychologically dangerous for the child and "horrific." Because it would be hard to say no to such sympathetic parents, we should simply not permit the case to arise. The embryo cloning issue of *Time* asks: "Or what about the couple that sets aside, as a matter of course, a clone of each of their children? If one of them died, the child could be replaced with a genetic equivalent" (8 November 1993, p. 68). *U.S. News & World Report* tells us that one of the most common cloning scenarios ethicists consider is parents cloning a child to replace a dying one (10 March 1997, p. 59). The *New York Times* asks us to consider "the case of a couple whose baby was dying and who wanted, literally, to replace the child" (24 February 1997: B8).

Many of these reports undercut their own efforts at genetic education by implying that the resulting child would in fact be a "replacement" while simultaneously quoting scientists and ethicists arguing against genetic determinism. But the most important aspect of this hypothetical is the idea that cloning is the kind of technology that would appeal to people who are pathologically unable to accept the fact of death. The reluctance to accept their loss leads them to create and use a second child (which they mistakenly see as a replacement) for their own comfort. Using the cloned child in this manner makes parents mild Kantian villains—creating a child as a means toward their own emotional ends. Interestingly, however, in very few of these discussions is there any mention of parents who already have other children following the death of a child, or even of the most common motivation to have children at all—to make parents' lives fuller and more rewarding. Looked at from a wider angle, it's not clear that these hypothetical parents are much different from any other parents, though they are described as particularly misguided.

We have been told implicitly and explicitly that the only motives for cloning adults are vicious.

The Organ-Donor Cloners. Another step up the ladder of using children as means to an end are those who would want to clone their children or themselves in order to save a life (an existing child's or their own). PBS's *Newshour* informs us that although clinical ethicists agree that it would be wrong to clone humans now, it might be permissible in the future once the safety question has been answered, for example in cases where a family needed a donor for a sick child. *Time* opens its special report with the hypothetical case of parents cloning a child to provide bone marrow for their leukemic daughter, telling us "the parents, who face the very likely prospect of losing the one daughter they have, could find themselves raising two of her—the second created expressly to help keep the first alive" (10 March 1997, p. 67).

In answering their own question of who would want to clone a human in the first place, *U.S. News & World Report* says: "to provide transplants for a dying child" (p. 59). It is not unreasonable, of course, to think that this might be attempted. As we have seen with the Ayalas' bone-marrow case, parents will have other children to save existing ones.[3] But in some reports this admittedly questionable means is rhetorically pushed into vague and scarier scenarios. The *New York Times* quotes Richard McCormick saying: "the obvious motives for cloning a human were 'the very reasons you should not.'" Concerned that people would use cloning to re-place dying children or create organ donors, he is also afraid it would tempt people toward eugenic engineering (1 March 1997, p. 10). The very first words in *Newsweek's* story on Dolly are: "[Biologist] Keith Campbell wasn't thinking, really, about rooms full of human clones, silently grow-ing spare parts for the person from whom they had been copied" (p. 53). In short, the supposition that people might clone a biological donor quickly makes its way toward eugenic dystopias, from *Nightline's* "babies produced in batches" to *Time's* intimation of an "embryo factory." In one of the very few cases where a bioethicist actually has space for a signifi-cant response to these hypotheticals, Ruth Macklin writes in *U.S. News & World Report:*

> Many of the science-fiction scenarios prompted by the prospect of human cloning turn out, upon reflection, to be absurdly improbable. There's the fear, for instance, that par-ents might clone a child to have "spare parts" in case the original child needs an organ transplant. But parents of identical twins don't view one child as an organ farm for the other. Why should cloned children's parents be any dif-ferent? . . . Banks stocked with the frozen sperm of geniuses already exist. They haven't created a master race because only a tiny number of women have wanted to impregnate themselves this way. Why think it will be different if hu-man cloning becomes available? (p. 64).

The Last-Chance-Infertile-Couple. Presented as the least objectionable motivation for seeking cloning is the case of the infertile couple who have tried all other treatments. Richard Nicholson, on *Nightline*, says the grotesque scenario of a dictator who wants copies of himself is unlikely. Instead, the more likely scenario is of a young infertile couple who after years of fertility treatment have had a child who is later struck down with meningitis. They know they can't have any more kids so they want to clone a child. *Time* claims that relieving the suffering of infertile couples is the "least controversial" aspect of cloning (8 November 1993, p. 67). *U.S. News & World Report* contrasts the megalomaniac who wants to be cloned to other cases where "adults might be tempted to clone themselves," in-cluding "a couple in which the man is infertile (who) might opt to clone one of them rather than introduce an outsider's sperm" (p. 61). While as a response to infertility, cloning may be "less controversial," these reports also strongly suggest that it is the medical status and extreme misfortune of infertile people that might justify the use of an otherwise suspect tech-nology. Cloning is treated only as a last resort for those who have failed in all the obviously better ways of procreating—maintaining cloning as a psy-chologically and morally inferior method of reproduction.

This summary of motivations for cloning demonstrates the extent to which we are already being trained to suspect anyone who might want to use the technique of pathological, pathetic, or gruesome tendencies. In fact, we have been told implicitly and explicitly that the only motives for cloning adults are vicious. *U.S. News & World Report* tells us "On adult cloning, ethicists are more united. . . . In fact the same commission that was divided on the issue of twins was unanimous in its conclusion that

cloning an adult's twin is 'bizarre . . . narcissistic and ethically impover-
ished'" (p. 61).

Brave new rhetoric

Cloning has not been reported as an unmitigated evil. The potential medical and agricultural benefits are usually mentioned. These benefits, however, are always juxtaposed to the dangers of cloning in alarmist, emo-
tion-packed ways—moderately useful medicines and improvements in
animal research versus a "brave new world."

Most people have never read *Brave New World,* but that doesn't matter. The scores of references to *Brave New World* aren't about the book;
they are about the trope connected to the book. *Brave New World* is a
stand-alone reference, image, and warning about dehumanization, total-
itarianism, and technology-wrought misery—epitomized and made possible by the technology of cloning. There is no comparable book that
praises cloning as a liberating technology. *Brave New World* stands alone,
framing the issue as a dichotomy between vaguely helpful medicine and
Fordist nightmares of enslaved and manufactured citizens. This easy and
morally non-neutral reference was a constant presence in clone report-
ing—along with more contemporary object lessons.

---

*We have been taught a morass of conflicting moral
and scientific lessons by the media's public
assessment of cloning.*

PBS's *Newshour* jumps from an explanation of cloning to a *Jurassic
Park* scene where a cloned T-rex terrorizes humans and then to a picture
of a copy of *Brave New World. Nightline* teases their story by saying,
"Tonight, cloning, dawn of a brave new world" and later asking if we are
"tiptoeing into the brave new world?" *Time* tells us: "A line had been
crossed. A taboo broken. A Brave New World of cookie-cutter humans,
baked and bred to order seemed . . . just over the horizon. Ethicists called
up nightmare visions of baby farming, of clones cannibalized for spare
parts" (8 November 1993, p. 65). Another issue warns us that, "The pos-
sibilities are as endless as they are ghastly: human hybrids, clone armies,
slave hatcheries, 'delta' and 'epsilon' sub-beings out of Aldous Huxley's
Brave New World" (10 March 1997, p. 61). Yet another *Time* tells us that
Neti and Ditto (the embryo-cloned rhesus monkeys) "were not so much
a step toward a brave new world as a diversion" (17 March 1997, p. 60).
U.S. News & World Report warns: "A world of clones and drones, of *The
Boys from Brazil* . . . was suddenly within reach" (p. 59). The references
continue, including the obligatory Frankenstein comparisons. But only
rarely do the assumptions get questioned, as when Bonnie Steinbock remarks on PBS that one misconception about cloning is *The Boys from
Brazil* scenario where clones are robotic and easily brainwashed. She says
cloning is nothing more than asexual reproduction and people usually
act frightened of anything new.

The reference to *Brave New World* in cloning reports is consistent with

Valerie Hartouni's analysis of its appearance in other reproductive technology debates. She writes:.

> In an otherwise diverse and contesting set of literatures spanning medicine, law, ethics, feminism, and public policy . . . *Brave New World* is a persistent and authoritative presence . . . the work is as frequently invoked only in passing or by title. In either case, the authority and centrality of the text are simply assumed, as is its relevance . . . Whether proffered as illustration, prophecy, or specter, invocations of Huxley's tale clearly function as a kind of shorthand for a host of issues having to do generally with the organization, application, and regulation of these new technologies.[4]

Seeding any discussion of cloning with apocalyptic, slippery slope anxiety, *Brave New World* and its contemporary offspring are treated as warnings by farsighted social critics more attuned to the dangers of science than naive or misguided scientists. This view of science is part and parcel of brave new rhetoric. Science may hold the answers to many important questions, but it is amoral and dangerous, and the scientists who give their lives to it are treated alternately as arrogant or naive. Article titles such as *Newsweek*'s "Little Lamb, Who Made Thee?" point toward scientists' intrusion on God's power, while at the same time exposing their political simplemindedness by writing:

> The Roslin scientists had no sooner trotted out Dolly than they assured everyone who asked that no one would ever, ever, apply the technology that made Dolly to humans. Pressed to answer whether human cloning was next, scientists prattled on about how immoral, illegal and pointless such a step would be. But as *The Guardian* pointed out, "Pointless, unethical and illegal things happen every day." (p. 57)

Time asks if science has finally "stepped over the line" in embryo cloning and assures us later with Dolly that it indeed has. *Time* then quotes Leon Kass: "Science is close to crossing some horrendous boundaries. . . . Here is an opportunity for human beings to decide if we're simply going to stand in the path of the technological steamroller or take control and help guide its direction" (10 March 1997, p. 70). PBS shows President Clinton warning scientists against "trying to play God."

While these hackneyed themes inevitably come up, one aspect of the commentaries appears to be different from other similar discussions. While repeatedly casting science as dangerous, and cloning as something that the "people" should stand up and refuse science permission to do, there is a recurring, reluctant admission that science is unstoppable and that human cloning is inevitable. *Newsweek* claims that Dolly's creation offers this lesson: "science, for better or worse, almost always wins; ethical qualms may throw some roadblocks in its path, or affect how widespread a technique becomes, but rarely is moral queasiness a match for the onslaught of science" (p. 59). This uncomfortable acquiescence to science and technology's presumed imperialism occurs again and again. A PBS interviewee says that all efforts to limit and regulate technological progress, including railroads and electricity and gunpowder have failed. Host Jim

Lehrer summarizes his point: "So if it's possible to clone human beings, human beings will be cloned." Charlie Rose says that there will always be private money to support this research and that government cannot stop it. The *New York Times* quotes Dr. Lee Silver saying that even if laws were in place to forbid cloning, clinics would crop up: "There's no way to stop it . . . Borders don't matter" (24 February 1997:B8). *Time* argues that we will not be able to stop cloning because the medical benefits are immense. *Newsweek* quotes Daniel Callahan saying: "In our society there are two values which will allow anyone to do whatever she wants in human reproduction . . . One is the nearly absolute right to reproduce—or not—as you see fit. The other is that just about anything goes in the pursuit of improved health" (p. 60). The collective message here seems to be that a brave new world is detestable, but may be unavoidable.

The moral of the copy

We have been taught a morass of conflicting moral and scientific lessons by the media's public assessment of cloning. But regardless of the consistency of smaller messages, the one idea that surfaces clearly is that we tread on the edge of disaster in attempting to copy ourselves. Though we may at times be comforted by biology lectures telling us that clones are not exact copies, the assumption that exact copies would in fact endanger us in some deep moral sense is very much alive. While no doubt this fear of the copy has a number of sources, I suspect one source is simply the sheer, age-old human desire to think of oneself as metaphysically special, possessing a unique mysterious spark of something that cannot be reduced, measured, or worst of all, copied. But this desire is exactly what science challenges, often unwittingly. If science can figure out enough about a human to be able to copy that human, to create a human, then it really has stepped over the line—but not so much a moral line as a line of privileging self-perception. This is the motivation behind the president's insistence that "each human life is unique, born of a miracle that reaches beyond laboratory science." Of course, this was said in the context of a speech banning federal funds for cloning, but it seems odd that we should make a law forbidding laboratory research if we really believe humans are mystical, mysterious, irreducibly miraculous beings. What could laboratory research do to that kind of being? What would be the point? The point is that cloning itself has its own message, an unsettling message that all good copies teach—the originals are not quite as special or mysterious as they thought.

Notes

1. In particular, I refer to these sources: *Time,* 8 November 1993, 10 March 1997, 17 March 1997; *U.S. News & World Report,* 10 March 1997; *Newsweek,* 10 March 1997; The *New York Times,* 24 February 1997, 25 February 1997, 1 March 1997; PBS's *Newshour* program; PBS's *The Charlie Rose Show;* ABC's *Nightline* program.

2. I already notice in my classes and in other groups that these examples are repeatedly cited as evidence that cloning can be put to no good use. The

hypotheticals and the presumed motivations of the characters are treated as certainties.

3. See Ronald Munson, *Reflection and Intervention* (Belmont, Calif.: Wadsworth, 1996).

4. See Valerie Hartouni, *"Brave New World* in the Discourses of Reproductive and Genetic Technologies," in *In the Nature of Things: Language, Politics, and the Environment,* ed. Jane Bennett and William Chaloupka (Minneapolis: University of Minnesota Press, 1993), pp. 86-87.

3

Human Cloning Is Inherently Unethical

E.V. Kontorovich

E.V. Kontorovich is a New York–based writer.

Advocates of human cloning stress its potential benefits but ignore the significant moral problems cloning would cause. Cloning takes the humanity out of reproduction, treats cloned humans as manufactured goods, and is similar to incest in the way it blurs and confuses family boundaries and relationships. Moreover, cloning as a scientific advance is unique in that it redefines humanity.

One year ago [February 1997], an obscure Scottish veterinarian named Ian Wilmut demonstrated how to make mammals, and by implication humans, in a laboratory without any act of sexual congress, indeed without sperm or an (intact) egg. Through cloning, a near-perfect genetic replica of a person could be grown from a single cell of skin, or, say, of rib. In the year since, cloning technology has developed rapidly. Experiments on cattle have refined the technique, and chimpanzee embryos have been successfully cloned. The possibility of human cloning now looms imminently, unseen but real.

When the cloned sheep, Dolly, first hit the newspapers, nearly 90 per cent of Americans found human cloning morally repugnant, according to every poll. Perhaps no other moral issue in American history has produced such near unanimity—not slavery, not Prohibition, not abortion. But politicians have been reluctant to cement this consensus into federal law.

A bill introduced in the Senate by Christopher Bond (R., Mo.) would have outlawed human cloning under a penalty of up to ten years in prison. It lost under a hail of criticism from medical groups, and even some conservative Republicans, that it would be an unnecessary impediment to scientific research. This is a seductive argument, especially when cancer victims like Sen. Connie Mack (R., Fla.) make it.

But the talk of concrete material benefits from cloning assumes that if it is permissible to reproduce certain cells for certain purposes (e.g., to reproduce a burn victim's remaining healthy skin cells to produce a graft), it is permissible to reproduce human beings in a Petrie dish.

Humans are embodied beings, our souls and physical selves are profoundly intertwined. Cloning would take the humanity out of human reproduction, and in so doing rob our spirits of something that cannot be replaced artificially. Furthermore, the manufacture of human beings on demand without conception would turn people into made-to-order goods, and would in aggregate debase our respect for human life.

Ignoring the moral arguments

Most advocates of cloning ignore the moral arguments and tempt us with small concrete benefits. These potential benefits—many of which, such as a cure for cancer, seem sheer fantasy—play on our current notions of rights and our culture of compassion in a way that gives them considerable political force. But these arguments constitute an end-run around the central issues. They do not sustain scrutiny.

There is little disagreement about the profound effects the cloning of human beings would have on human nature. However, some cloning apologists simply respond, "So what?" For example, Harvard Law professor Laurence Tribe sees flaws in "a society that bans acts of human creation for no better reason than that their particular form defies nature and tradition." Princeton molecular biologist Lee Silver makes a stronger case than many critics do, that cloning would completely redefine human life, but embraces this outcome as a way for us to take control of our destiny as a species and reshape it as we see fit.

We hear most often that cloning could provide perfectly compatible body parts for persons who need them or that it could enable infertile couples and homosexuals to have "biological" offspring. It is hard to say without sounding callous, but death and bodily infirmity are concomitant with human existence and in the long run unavoidable. We live in a society where longevity is becoming a value in itself, but longevity cannot justify a practice that is basically wrong.

As for infertility, it is not even a disabling sickness that, on humanitarian grounds, we should feel obliged to alleviate. It is simply a limitation, on the order of not being tall or wealthy. There is nothing heartless about saying that people should resort to alternatives besides cloning, like adoption. As for those whose arguments are informed by the belief that people have a right to make use of whatever new technologies become available, even Laurence Tribe concedes that there can be no such general right.

Cloning nightmares

When defenders of cloning talk about the brave new world of medical techniques they skip over the fact that its most wondrous manufactures would be Calibans. Consider the likeliest way in which cloning can be used to help with illness: through the creation of perfectly compatible organs for transplantation. It is important here to remember what cloning entails: the DNA-laden nucleus from a somatic (body) cell is placed into a denucleated egg and stimulated into growth with an electric shock. What begins to grow is a "fertilized" egg, an embryo—not a kidney or any other disembodied piece of tissue.

Charles Krauthammer wrote about experiments at the University of Texas in which headless mice were created, and raised the specter of headless humans used as organ factories: "there is no grosser corruption of biotechnology than creating a human mutant and disemboweling it for spare parts." Actually, there is perhaps one grosser corruption, for the "headless human" scenario is still a science fiction nightmare: it is much easier to delete mouse genes (preventing the head from growing) than human genes. In the meantime, cloned organs would probably have to develop within human fetuses, which would be aborted when the organs were ready.

This is called "organ farming": growing human life as material. Advocates of cloning like to sidestep the idea of organ farming with visions of growing organs, not a fetus. Such techniques, while theoretically possible, are entirely speculative. There is no reason to believe they will ever be perfected. And, in any case, work with higher-order animals (not banned in any of the bills) would allow such research to continue.

There is little disagreement about the profound effects the cloning of human beings would have on human nature.

The infertility applications of cloning have nightmares of their own. Consider: a woman wants "biological" children, but her ovaries do not work because of age or other reasons. She clones herself. The fetus will be female, and have inside her ovaries a lifetime supply of eggs, exactly identical to the woman's own eggs. The fetus is then aborted and the eggs harvested for implantation in the woman. This is an option actually entertained by some fertility doctors, who say they already see a market for it; cloning defenders like Professor Silver celebrate this as a marvelous extension of a woman's reproductive capabilities.

The fact that people are already inventing—and endorsing—such scenarios demonstrates the corrosive magic this technology works on the notion of human dignity. Indeed, it is not just the horrific applications but cloning itself that are abominations. For human beings are unavoidably defined by our biological, embodied natures. How we come into being is not trivial: it is central to who we are. This is one of the reasons why incest, even consensual incest—which like cloning, has no "victims"—offends us to our core. It blurs the lines of kinship: the begotten couples with her begetter.

AND if incest crosses the boundaries defined by the human way of coming into being, cloning twists and breaks them. Parents and children would be replaced with "donors" and "clones." The relationship between the parties to asexual reproduction would be inherently ambiguous (the species which currently practice it, amoebas and the like, show zero interest in their relatives). But that relationship surely would be affected by the fact that cloning constitutes the manufacture of humans as made-to-order goods. The danger is that if people are made and not begotten, they become like everything else which is but a tool: a means, not an end.

Some writers, like Harvard biology professor Richard Lewontin, say all the furor is over nothing. Clones are no different from twins, they say, so what's the big deal? Well, what was the last pair of twins heard of born fifty years apart to two different women? What woman who gives birth to a handsome child can go to a doctor and request another genetically identical one, or maybe a dozen? The real moral issue is not the genetic make-up of clones, but the method of their manufacture. It is asexual reproduction that robs a cloned child of parents, not the fact that someone else shares his genotype.

Some people, of course, have no patience for arguments about morality and justice, and care only about ruddy, healthy human beings. But even they should reject cloning. In individual cases, cloning may benefit some, but it will be a very selfish advance because in the long run it undermines the advancement of the human species. There is good reason that all higher life forms are reproduced through random combinations of two mates' DNA. The constant changes in genotype create the variety necessary for the species to respond to environmental changes. Since the environment is constantly changing, failure to vary the genotype creates genetic stagnation that can be catastrophic.

We've become accustomed to revolutionary technologies emerging daily, from microchips to surgical lasers. But even the most advanced technologies merely facilitate or improve upon normal human functions. While cloning may look just like a particularly impressive piece of laboratory wizardry, actually it redefines the parameters of human life. Such breakthroughs do not happen every day.

However, one thing we can say about cloning is that it is an entirely new transgression. Unfortunately, since Eve was beguiled by the serpent, mankind has never been good at understanding sin without experiencing it.

4

Human Cloning Is Not Inherently Unethical

Raymond K. DeHainaut

Raymond K. DeHainaut teaches international studies at the University of South Florida and is associate editor of The Human Quest. *He was previously a Methodist missionary in the Dominican Republic.*

Anti-abortion activists and other conservatives who condemn human cloning and call for banning it are mistaken in assuming it is always wrong. People may be cloned for ethical or unethical motives, but there is nothing inherently wrong with cloning itself. Cloning has power to bring much good *or* much evil to the human race, depending on how it is used.

No sooner had Dolly, the cloned sheep appeared on the cover of *Time* magazine, and even before G. Richard Seed's announcement that he had decided to use this proven technology to clone a human being in the near future, President Clinton got the jump on even the most conservative, anti-abortionist and anti-scientific nay-sayers in calling for a moratorium on the use of federal funds for human-cloning research. In his 1998 State of the Union message, he called for legislation to totally ban human cloning. Congress has not yet passed such legislation, but the Food and Drug Administration has recently announced that it has the authority to regulate human cloning and that it would be a violation of federal law to try the procedure without its approval. That means that anyone, such as Mr. Seed, who plans to attempt human cloning, must file a formal application under the rubric of genetic therapy and be subjugated to an endless labyrinth of red tape. On January 19, 1998, representatives from 19 European countries signed an agreement to ban human cloning.

It is possible that some of this political-populist paranoia might slow down the application of cloning technology to humans, but in no way will it permanently block the inevitable. Seed has already said that if the US government moves to block his plans, he will move his operation to some foreign country that has no such prohibitions. Some suspect that Seed may not have the technical ability to carry out his plans, but the

Reprinted from "Are Those Who Would Ban Cloning Wrong?" by Raymond K. DeHainaut, *The Human Quest*, May/June 1998. Reprinted by permission.

technology is there and it will eventually be applied by someone somewhere. Seed may not be another Copernicus or Galileo, but he has to confront the same kind of scare tactics and medieval mentality.

Those who have been so quick to follow the sensationalist press and criminalize human cloning have not demonstrated any real interest in looking at the issue from an ethical point of view. Church agencies such as the United Methodist Board of Church and Society have also been quick to jump on board with "politically correct" condemnations of human cloning. From a purely ethical point of view, it is difficult to see what is "wrong" with cloning a human being. A human clone is just a time-delayed identical twin of another person, perhaps one or the other of a married couple.

From a purely ethical point of view, it is difficult to see what is "wrong" with cloning a human being.

Of course ethics do come into play in that a woman giving birth to a clone would have to be acting voluntarily. If it is the husband who is to be cloned, it is possible that the wife might have reservations about giving birth to her husband's twin brother and might not want to do so. But, on the other hand, she might welcome her husband's clone completely free of genetic conditions common in her own gene pool.

Ethical considerations also oblige us to look at possible positive results from human cloning. This cloning may quickly make it possible to produce specific human tissues. The magazine *The New Scientist* (May 31, 1997) points out that "If such research could help cure Parkinson's disease or repair damaged spines, then the benefits appear to outweigh any moral repugnance we have about cloning human tissue."

Also on the positive side, in addition to avoiding and repairing diseases and deformities carried by genes, would be the possibility of programming better genetic characteristics. The gifted individuals, representing a small portion of humanity famed for their abilities, theories, inventions and discoveries that have contributed to the betterment of society could be cloned in larger numbers. Of course, this would have to be done under careful ethical supervision in order to avoid any misguided attempts to produce a "Master Race." Someone has jokingly remarked that we wouldn't want to clone too many Bill Gates, as this would produce an oversupply of billionaires in the world. All joking aside, the question of cloning needs to be approached with the same kind of ethical concerns that have been applied to nuclear technology. Questions have to be asked about who is going to be doing the cloning and about who will be cloned. No one is suggesting that all caution should be thrown to the winds. It will just be a matter of time until a cloned human being will appear alongside of Dolly the sheep, and the calves recently cloned, despite national and international prohibitions. But this is not to say that national or international agreements should not be sought to prevent reckless experimentation and the production of cloned human zombies for spare body parts.

But the ethical answer is not to be found in nearsighted, kneejerk prohibitions. A number of US congressional representatives have already announced that they will soon introduce legislation to put strict limits on cloning. These conservative legislators have already caused several scientific groups to express their concern that some of the bills aimed at preventing human cloning might also prohibit other kinds of cloning that involves humans, but could benefit the future of humankind. Fortunately, cloning in general has not yet been banned in Boston, allowing for the recent birth or appearance of George and Charlie, the first calves to be cloned by two Massachusetts scientists. Among the first payoffs from genetically engineered cattle is that they will be able to secrete serum of human albumen in their milk from cross-over genes and other pharmaceutical drugs. A similar cloning and gene-splicing technique in pigs could make it possible to transplant pig organs into humans, thus saving human lives.

Cloning and religion

Of course, there are many Bible thumpers and conservative theologians who will argue that those who clone or do research in cloning are presumptuous sinners interfering with God's work and God's creation. These are usually the same people who have come out against evolution and abortion. The anti-abortionists who are against human cloning must be somewhat confused over this issue. They say that life begins at conception. But considering that conception does not take place in human cloning, would the abortion of a cloned fetus, then, become permissible for them? A friend of mine recently pointed out that just a cell from any part of a human can fertilize the female's egg and a sperm is not needed. The anti-abortionists say that life begins at conception. But as he told me in a letter, "Because any bit of genetic material can be used (such as that flaking off my fingers as I type this) does this mean that we must save all flesh and not just the fertilized ovum?"

One could argue that God would not have given humanity the knowledge . . . [of] the techniques of cloning if they could not be used for the benefit of human kind.

My friend and I also agreed that just as the conservative traditionalist critics of Copernicus and Galileo had it wrong, the critics of cloning today also have it wrong. However, it is encouraging to know that not all religious leaders and representatives of churches have joined the nay-sayers. Mr. Seed who started all of this controversy when he announced his intention to clone human beings is himself an active member of a Protestant church in Illinois, and his own pastor has publicly announced that "He is doing this out of compassion." From a theological point of view, one could argue that God would not have given humanity the knowledge and ability to come up with the techniques of cloning if they could not be used for the benefit of human kind. The ability to launch rockets into space could also be condemned because it enables us to make intercontinental ballistic missiles. But it also gives us the ability to explore new worlds.

5

Cloning Could Place an Unfair Burden on Clones

Søren Holm

Søren Holm is a senior research fellow in the Department of Medical Philosophy and Clinical Theory, Faculty of Health Sciences, at the University of Copenhagen, Denmark.

People who are cloned would be perceived as copies and would live their lives "in the shadow" of the original genetic donor. Human cloning is morally problematic for this reason.

O ne of the arguments that is often put forward in the discussion of human cloning is that it is in itself wrong to create a copy of a human being.
This argument is usually dismissed by pointing out that a) we do not find anything wrong in the existence of monozygotic twins even though they are genetically identical, and b) the clone would not be an exact copy of the original even in those cases where it is an exact genetic copy, since it would have experienced a different environment that would have modified its biological and psychological development.

In my view both these counterarguments are valid, but nevertheless I think that there is some core of truth in the assertion that it is wrong deliberately to try to create a copy of an already existing human being. It is this idea that I will briefly try to explicate here.

The life in the shadow argument

When we see a pair of monozygotic twins who are perfectly identically dressed some of us experience a slight sense of unease, especially in the cases where the twins are young children. This unease is exacerbated when people establish competitions where the winners are the most identical pair of twins. The reason for this uneasiness is, I believe, that the identical clothes could signal a reluctance on the part of the parents to let each twin develop his or her individual and separate personality or a reluctance to let each twin lead his or her own life. In the extreme case each twin is constantly compared with the other and any difference is counteracted.

In the case of cloning based on somatic cells we have what is effectively a set of monozygotic twins with a potentially very large age difference. The original may have lived all his or her life and may even have died before the clone is brought into existence. Therefore, there will not be any direct day-by-day comparison and identical clothing, but then a situation that is even worse for the clone is likely to develop. I shall call this situation "a life in the shadow" and I shall develop an argument against human cloning that may be labeled the "life in the shadow argument."

Let us try to imagine what will happen when a clone is born and its social parents have to begin rearing it. Usually when a child is born we ask hypothetical questions like "How will it develop?" or "What kind of person will it become?" and we often answer them with reference to various psychological traits we think we can identify in the biological mother or father or in their families, for instance "I hope that he won't get the kind of temper you had when you were a child!"

There is some core of truth in the assertion that it is wrong deliberately to try to create a copy of an already existing human being.

In the case of the clone we are, however, likely to give much more specific answers to such questions. Answers that will then go on to affect the way the child is reared. There is no doubt that the common public understanding of the relationship between genetics and psychology contains substantial strands of genetic essentialism, i.e., the idea that the genes determine psychology and personality.[1] This public idea is reinforced every time the media report the finding of new genes for depression, schizophrenia, etc. Therefore, it is likely that the parents of the clone will already have formed in their minds a quite definite picture of how the clone will develop, a picture that is based on the actual development of the original. This picture will control the way they rear the child. They will try to prevent some developments, and try to promote others. Just imagine how a clone of Adolf Hitler or Pol Pot would be reared, or how a clone of Albert Einstein, Ludwig van Beethoven, or Michael Jordan would be brought up. The clone would in a very literal way live his or her life in the shadow of the life of the original. At every point in the clone's life there would be someone who had already lived that life, with whom the clone could be compared and against whom the clone's accomplishments could be measured.

That there would in fact be a strong tendency to make the inference from genotype to phenotype and to let the conclusion of such an inference affect rearing can perhaps be seen more clearly if we imagine the following hypothetical situation:

> In the future new genetic research reveals that there are only a limited number of possible human genotypes, and that genotypes are therefore recycled every 300 years (i.e., somebody who died 300 years ago had exactly the same genotype

as me). It is further discovered that there is some complicated, but not practically impossible, method whereby it is possible to discover the identity of the persons who 300, 600, 900, etc. years ago instantiated the genotype that a specific fetus now has.

I am absolutely certain that people would split into two sharply disagreeing camps if this became a possibility. One group, perhaps the majority, would try to identify the previous instantiations of their child's genotype. Another group would emphatically not seek this information because they would not want to know and would not want their children to grow up in the shadow of a number of previously led lives with the same genotype. The option to remain in ignorance is, however, not open to social parents of contemporary clones.

If the majority would seek the information in this scenario, firms offering the method of identification would have a very brisk business, and it could perhaps even become usual to expect of prospective parents that they make use of this new possibility. Why would this happen? The only reasonable explanation, apart from initial curiosity, is that people would believe that by identifying the previous instantiation of the genotype they would thereby gain valuable knowledge about their child. But knowledge is in general only valuable if it can be converted into new options for action, and the most likely form of action would be that information about the previous instantiations would be used in deciding how to rear the present child. This again points to the importance of the public perception of genetic essentialism, since the environment must have changed considerably in the 300-year span between each instantiation of the genotype.

What is wrong about a life in the shadow?

What is wrong with living your life as a clone in the shadow of the life of the original? It diminishes the clone's possibility of living a life that is in a full sense of that word his or her life. The clone is forced to be involved in an attempt to perform a complicated partial re-enactment of the life of somebody else (the original). In our usual arguments for the importance of respect for autonomy or for the value of self-determination we often affirm that it is the final moral basis for these principles that they enable persons to live their lives the way they themselves want to live these lives. If we deny part of this opportunity to clones and force them to live their lives in the shadow of someone else we are violating some of our most fundamental moral principles and intuitions. Therefore, as long as genetic essentialism is a common cultural belief there are good reasons not to allow human cloning.

Final qualifications

It is important to note that the 'life in the shadow argument' does not rely on the false premise that we can make an inference from genotype to (psychological or personality) phenotype, but only on the true premise that there is a strong public tendency to make such an inference. This means that the conclusions of the argument only follow as long as this empirical premise remains true. If ever the public relinquishes all belief in genetic essentialism the 'life in the shadow argument' would fail, but such a development seems highly unlikely.

The attraction in cloning for many is exactly in the belief that I can recreate myself.

In conclusion I should perhaps also mention that I am fully aware of two possible counterarguments to the argument presented above. The first points out that even if a life in the shadow of the original is perhaps problematic and not very good, it is the only life the clone can have, and that it is therefore in the clone's interest to have this life as long as it is not worse than having no life at all. The 'life in the shadow argument' therefore does not show that cloning should be prohibited. I am unconvinced by this counterargument, just as I am by all arguments involving comparisons between existence and nonexistence, but it is outside the scope of the present short paper to show decisively that the counterargument is wrong.

The second counterargument states that the conclusions of the 'life in the shadow argument' can be avoided if all clones are anonymously put up for adoption, so that no knowledge about the original is available to the social parents of the clone. I am happy to accept this counterargument, but I think that a system where I was not allowed to rear the clone of myself would practically annihilate any interest in human cloning. The attraction in cloning for many is exactly in the belief that I can recreate myself. The cases where human cloning solves real medical or reproductive problems are on the fringe of the area of cloning.

Note

1. Nelkin D, Lindee MS. *The DNA Mystique: The Gene as a Cultural Icon.* New York: W.H. Freeman and Company, 1995.

6

A Clone Can Exist with Full Human Dignity

Timothy J. Madigan

Timothy J. Madigan is editor of Free Inquiry, *a humanist journal.*

Human clones would be unique and special persons with the same human rights and qualities that all other people possess. It is opponents of cloning who threaten to stigmatize clones as copies or monsters. Society will have to protect the equality of clones.

> All truth passes through three stages. First it is ridiculed. Second it is violently opposed. Third it is accepted as being self-evident.
> —*Arthur Schopenhauer (1788–1860)*

I was a student at a Catholic high school in 1978 when the first successful *in vitro* fertilization case occurred, and I well remember the storm of controversy it caused. The events that ensued at the time met Schopenhauer's dictum above. First, comics like Johnny Carson had a field day telling jokes about "test-tube babies." Then several institutions, including the Catholic Church, began denouncing the procedure for being an act against nature. After the birth of Louise Brown though, things quieted down, and now the procedure is relatively routine. The United States alone has almost 300 *in vitro* fertilization clinics. Now, 20 years later, a new debate is following along the same lines.

The notion of cloning human beings seems to have passed from Schopenhauer's first stage (remember all the "Hello, Dolly!" jokes when Ian Wilmut announced in February 1997 that he had successfully cloned a lamb from an adult sheep) to the second stage. The U. S. Congress is debating whether all research on *human* cloning should be outlawed, and religious organizations of various denominations have urged them to do so. Meanwhile, Dr. Richard Seed has announced that he will open a clinic for this very procedure. As with *in vitro* clinics, where federal funding for research has long been banned, it is likely that private finance will fill in the gap. Indeed, the Raelians, a bizarre UFO religion based in Switzerland,

Reprinted from "Cloning and Human Dignity," by Timothy J. Madigan, *Free Inquiry*, Summer 1997. Reprinted with permission.

has offered to fund Dr. Seed in his efforts. Talk about strange bedfellows!

Free Inquiry has been in the forefront of this debate, issuing a "Declaration in Defense of Cloning and the Integrity of Scientific Research" in its Summer 1997 issue. Signed by such luminaries as DNA codiscoverer Francis Crick, famed philosopher W.V. Quine, and biologist Richard Dawkins, the declaration was mentioned in articles in the *New York Times, Der Spiegel,* and several syndicated services. At the time, *Free Inquiry* was something of a lone voice in urging that inflammatory and ill-considered talk about "Frankenstein's monster" coming to life be halted and a better understanding of the implications and consequences of cloning be addressed.

In December 1997, 19 members of the Council of Europe signed a treaty against cloning, primarily because it is "contrary to human dignity and thus constitutes a misuse of biology and medicine." Interestingly enough, Britain—where the first test-tube baby was born, and where Dolly was introduced—did not sign the treaty. It has a strong tradition of defending the freedom of scientific research.

The need to defend human dignity is central to the humanist position. But in my view, it is the *opponents* of human cloning who are laying the groundwork for discrimination and prejudicial treatment. The main point to keep in mind is that a cloned human being would *not* be a mere replicant. It would be a unique person. Clones would essentially be *delayed* identical twins, with the added benefit that it is unlikely that each twin would have to suffer being dressed in the same fashions, as contemporary twins so often are. Yet the chorus of voices coming from opponents of the procedure are already placing a stigma upon this potential group, referring to them as "monsters" or mere "carbon copies." Much like the stigma placed on "illegitimate" children over the centuries, it is this very negative attitude that will be the most likely cause of an affront to human dignity, by marginalizing an entire group of people solely due to the manner of their birth.

As far as I know, so-called test-tube babies have not been victims of this sort of stigmatization, and I hope that the same general acceptance will be given to the first cloned infants. While public debate is necessary for such a monumental change, the rhetoric needs to be toned down, to prevent creating a caste system based on birth.

In my view, it is the opponents *of human cloning who are laying the groundwork for discrimination and prejudicial treatment.*

Gina Kolata, in her recent book examining the controversy (*Clone: The Road to Dolly, and the Path Ahead,* New York: William Morrow & Company, 1998), points out that Wilmut was able to do his research unhampered precisely *because* the orthodox view was that adult cloning was pure science fiction, without any real chance of occurring. In 1984, for instance, the highly respected embryologist Davor Solter and his student James McGrath wrote an article in *Science* magazine, authoritatively stating: "the cloning of mammals, by simple nuclear transfer, is biologically impossible." Scientists more than anyone should be careful in ruling out the very possibility of technological progress. While a few medical ethicists like the humanist scholar Joseph Fletcher tried to prepare society for a rational discussion of the issue, clearly almost everyone was unprepared for the shock of Dolly's entrance into the world. What will make human cloning a reality is not the machinations of research scientists, though. It is the public demand of human beings who want to use this technology to have children.

The defense of human dignity will come from how the cloned individuals are loved and respected by their parents, their peers, and their society.

While mammalian cloning has been successful, it remains to be seen if human beings will be able to benefit from this. But if it does occur, and if we are to move toward Schopenhauer's third stage of general acceptance, this stage must be set for welcoming such beings as unique and special persons, not mere copies or "monsters." Ultimately, as it is with all other humans, the defense of human dignity will come from how the cloned individuals are loved and respected by their parents, their peers, and their society. Schopenhauer, who felt that romantic love was merely nature's way of duping us into reproducing our species, might be appalled by yet another means of doing so. But those who desire this procedure are surely motivated primarily by the desire to raise a child. Indeed, cloned infants will by and large meet the criteria of being "wanted" by their parents. It will be up to all of us to make sure that society as a whole treats them with equal respect.

7

Only Married Couples
Should Be Allowed to Clone

James Q. Wilson

James Q. Wilson is emeritus professor at the University of California at Los Angeles and author of Crime and Human Nature, Moral Judgment, *and other books.*

Cloning can be viewed as simply another form of assisted reproduction like artificial insemination and in vitro fertilization. The important point to consider in protecting the child's welfare is not how the child was created, but the family in which he or she is raised. Therefore, cloning should be limited to intact heterosexual families and restrictions should be placed on the sources of human eggs. With such restrictions in place, cloning is unlikely to become very common.

Like most people, I instinctively recoil from the idea of cloning human beings. But we ought to pause and identify what in the process is so distressing. My preliminary view is that the central problem is not creating an identical twin but creating it without parents. Children born of a woman—however the conception is produced—will in the great majority of cases enjoy that special irrational affection that has been vital to human upbringings for millennia. If she is married to a man and they, like the great majority of married couples, invest energy, love, and commitment in the child, the child is likely to do well.

My argument is that the structure of the family a child is born into is more important than the sexual process by which the child is produced. If Leon Kass and other opponents of cloning think that sexuality is more important than families, they should object to any form of assisted reproduction that does not involve parental coition. Many such forms now exist. Children are adopted by parents who did not give them birth. Artificial insemination produces children without sexual congress. Some forms of such insemination rely on sperm produced by a man other than the woman's husband, while other forms involve the artificial insemination of a surrogate mother who will relinquish the baby to a married

Reprinted from "The Ethics of Human Cloning," by James Q. Wilson, *The American Enterprise*, March/April 1999. Reprinted by permission.

couple. By *in vitro* fertilization, eggs and sperm can be joined in a Petri dish and then transferred into the woman's uterus.

I have mixed views about assisted reproduction. Some forms I endorse, others I worry about, still others I oppose. The two principles on which my views rest concern, first, the special relationship between infant and mother that is the product of childbirth, however conception was arranged, and second, the great advantage to children that comes from growing up in an intact, two-parent family.

Assisted reproduction, whether by artificial insemination or *in vitro* fertilization, is now relatively common. In none of those cases is the child the result of marital sex. And in some cases the child is not genetically related to at least one parent. I am aware of no study that shows *in vitro* fertilization to have harmed the children's mental or psychological status or their relationships with parents. A study in England compared children conceived by *in vitro* fertilization, or by artificial insemination with sperm from an unknown donor, with children who were sexually conceived and grew up in either birth or adoptive families. By every measure of parenting, the children who were the product of either an artificial fertilization or insemination by a donor did better than children who were naturally conceived. The better parenting should not be surprising. Those parents had been struggling to have children; when a new technology made it possible, they were delighted, and that delight motivated them to be especially supportive of their offspring.

Some observers are opposed to all of these arrangements, no matter what their effect on children. Paul Ramsey argued in 1970 that for any third party—say, an egg or sperm donor—to be involved violates the marriage covenant. That is also the view of the Roman Catholic Church. My view is different: If the child is born of a woman who is part of a two-parent family, and both parents work hard to raise him or her properly, we poor mortals have done all that man and God might expect of us.

The structure of the family a child is born into is more important than the sexual process by which the child is produced.

Matters become more complex when a surrogate mother is involved. There, a woman is inseminated by a man so that she may bear a child to be given to another couple. That process uses a woman's body from the start for purposes against which her own instincts, as well as our own moral judgments, rebel.

The case of Baby M in New Jersey began with a child born to Mary Beth Whitehead. She had entered into a contractual agreement with William and Elizabeth Stern to deliver the child to them. Mrs. Whitehead had become pregnant through artificial fertilization by Mr. Stern's sperm. After the baby's birth, Mrs. Whitehead refused to surrender it; the Sterns sued. The judge decided that the contract should be honored and the baby should go to the Sterns. On appeal, the New Jersey Supreme Court decided unanimously that the contract was invalid but gave the baby to Mr. Stern and allowed Mrs. Whitehead visiting rights.

The contract, according to the court, was void because it illegally used money to procure a child. More importantly, because no woman can truly give informed consent to relinquishing an infant she has not yet borne and seen, Mrs. Whitehead had not entered into a valid contract. At that time, and so far as I know even today, in every state but Wyoming no woman can agree to allowing her child to be adopted unless that agreement is ratified after birth.

I favor limiting cloning to intact, heterosexual families.

Why, then, did the court give the child to Mr. Stern? The court did not like Mrs. Whitehead. She was poor, ill-educated, moved frequently, received public assistance, and was married to an alcohol abuser. To me, Mrs. Whitehead's condition was largely irrelevant. The central fact was that she was the baby's mother. The overwhelming body of biological and anthropological evidence supports the view that women become deeply attached to their children. The mother-child bond is one of the most powerful in nature and is essential to the existence, to say nothing of the health, of human society.

The child belonged to its mother, period. That does not mean that all forms of surrogate mothering are wrong, but it at least means that the buyer of the surrogate's services is completely at risk. Given that risk, surrogate motherhood will never become popular, but it will occur in some cases.

I favor limiting cloning to intact, heterosexual families and placing sharp restrictions on the source of the eggs. We do not want families planning to have a movie star, basketball player, or high-energy physicist as an offspring. But I confess I am not clear as to how those limits might be drawn, and if no one can solve that puzzle, I would join Kass in banning cloning. Perhaps the best solution is a kind of screened lottery akin to what doctors performing *in vitro* fertilization now do with donated sperm. One can match his race or ethnicity and even select a sex, but beyond that he takes his chances.

I am persuaded that if only married couples can clone, and if we sharply limit the sources of the embryo they can implant in the woman, cloning will be quite rare. Sex is more fun than cloning, and artificial insemination and *in vitro* fertilization preserve the element of genetic chance that most people, I think, favor. Dr. Kass is right to stress the mystery and uncertainty of sexual union. That is why hardly any woman with a fertile husband who could obtain sperm from a donor bank will do so. Procreation is a delight.

8

Cloning Human Embryos for Medical Purposes Is Unethical

William Keeler

William Keeler is a Roman Catholic cardinal and archbishop of Baltimore. He spoke against cloning before a congressional committee on February 12, 1998.

The cloning of human embryos for the sole purpose of medical research and cell cultivation is an unethical practice that should be opposed. A ban on such human cloning research would stimulate alternative methods that do not create, exploit, and destroy human lives.

I am Cardinal William Keeler, archbishop of Baltimore and a member of the Committee for Pro-Life Activities of the National Conference of Catholic Bishops. It is on behalf of this conference that I speak to you today about the moral challenge presented by human cloning.

The sanctity and dignity of human life is a cornerstone of Catholic moral reflection and social teaching. We believe a society can be judged by the respect it shows for human life, especially in its most vulnerable stages and conditions.

On this basis the Catholic Church strongly opposes the taking of human life through abortion, euthanasia or destructive experiments on human embryos.

The dehumanizing nature of cloning

At first glance, human cloning may not seem to belong on this list. It is presented as a means for creating life, not destroying it. Yet it shows disrespect toward human life in the very act of generating it. Cloning completely divorces human reproduction from the context of a loving union between man and woman, producing children with no "parents" in the

Testimony given by Cardinal William Keeler before the House Commerce Committee's Subcommittee on Health and the Environment, February 12, 1998, Washington, D.C.

ordinary sense. Here human life does not arise from an act of love, but is manufactured to predetermined specifications. A developing human being is treated as an object, not as an individual with his or her own identity and rights. As one group of scientific and other experts advising the Holy See has written:

"In the cloning process the basic relationships of the human person are perverted: filiation, consanguinity, kinship, parenthood. A woman can be the twin sister of her mother, lack a biological father and be the daughter of her grandmother. In vitro fertilization has already led to the confusion of parentage, but cloning will mean the radical rupture of these bonds."[1]

Human embryos—produced without true parents and hence without protectors—would be created at the outset for the sole purpose of experimentation and destruction.

Such moral concern transcends denominational bounds and has been eloquently expressed by some of our country's most respected philosophers and ethicists. Writes Professor Leon Kass of the University of Chicago:

"Human cloning would . . . represent a giant step toward turning begetting into making, procreation into manufacture (literally, something *handmade*) . . . [W]e here would be taking a major step into making man himself simply another one of the man-made things."[2]

From the dehumanizing nature of this technique flow many disturbing consequences. Because human clones are produced by a means more suited to more primitive forms of life—a means which involves no loving relationship, no personal investment or responsibility for a new life but only laboratory technique—they would be uniquely at risk of being treated as "second-class" human beings.

The very scenarios often cited as justifications for human cloning are actually symptoms of the moral problem it creates. It has been said that cloning could be used to create "copies" of illustrious people, or to replace a deceased loved one, or even to provide a source of spare tissues or organs for the person whose genetic material was used for the procedure. In each proposal we see a utilitarian view of human life in which a human being is treated as a means to someone else's ends instead of as a person with his or her own inherent dignity. This same attitude lies at the root of human slavery.

Let me be perfectly clear. In reality a cloned human being would not be in any sense an "object" or a substandard human being. Whatever the circumstances of his or her origin, he or she deserves to be treated as a human person with an individual identity. But the depersonalized technique of manufacture known as cloning disregards this dignity and sets the stage for further exploitation. Cloning is not wrong because cloned human beings lack human dignity—it is wrong because they *have* human dignity and deserve to come into the world in ways that respect this dignity. Each child has a right to be conceived and born as the fruit of a loving union between husband and wife, to be loved and accepted as a new and distinct individual.

Cloning and human embryo research

Ironically, the most startling evidence of the dehumanizing aspects of cloning is found in some proposals ostensibly aimed at preventing human cloning. The National Bioethics Advisory Commission and now some members of Congress favor legislation that would not ban human cloning at all—but would simply ban any effort to allow cloned human beings to survive. In these proposals researchers are allowed to use cloning for the unlimited mass production of human embryos for experimentation—after which they are required to destroy them instead of allowing them to implant in a woman's womb.[3]

Enactment of such a proposal would mark the first time in history that the U.S. government defined a class of human beings that it is a crime *not* to destroy. These human embryos—produced without true parents and hence without protectors—would be created at the outset for the sole purpose of experimentation and destruction.

Human embryo research has been debated in this body before. In 1994 the National Institutes of Health proposed that federally funded researchers be allowed to perform nontherapeutic experiments on human embryos produced by in vitro fertilization—including embryos produced solely for research purposes. The moral outcry against this proposal was almost universal. Opinion polls showed massive opposition, and the NIH panel making the recommendation was inundated with over 50,000 letters of protest. The *Washington Post,* while reaffirming its stand in favor of legalized abortion, editorialized against the panel's recommendation:

"The creation of human embryos specifically for research that will destroy them is unconscionable . . . . [I]t is not necessary to be against abortion rights or to believe human life literally begins at conception to be deeply alarmed by the notion of scientists purposely causing conceptions in a context entirely divorced from even the potential of reproduction."[4]

Creating human life solely to cannibalize and destroy it is the most unconscionable use of human cloning.

President Clinton ultimately set aside the recommendation allowing creation of "research embryos," and Congress for the past three years has voted to prohibit funding of all harmful embryo research—most especially the creation of research embryos.

Why then are these moral judgments suddenly reversed if the human embryo has been produced by cloning? Why is Congress now being urged to endorse the proposition: "The creation of human embryos by cloning specifically for research that will destroy them is a national priority"? It seems the cloning procedure is so demeaning that people somehow assume that a brief life as an object of research, followed by destruction, is "good enough" for any human produced by this technique. The fact that the procedure invites such morally irresponsible policies is reason enough to oppose it.

The National Bioethics Advisory Commission approach does not even make sense as a barrier to cloning for reproductive purposes. For a great deal of destructive experimentation using cloned human embryos would be a necessary step toward the production of a live-born infant by cloning. We have all learned that as many as 276 sheep embryos, fetuses and newborn lambs had to die so that one sheep, "Dolly," could be produced. Scientists can expect similar results from initial attempts at human cloning—indicating that it would be morally irresponsible to make the attempt. Yet legislation based on the NBAC approach would give the federal government's blessing to such experiments. Researchers who discard hundreds or thousands of human embryos in failed cloning attempts could resort to the defense that such cavalier disposal of human life is exactly what the federal law requires.

Religious views?

Some will ask, By speaking here of a human embryo, let alone a human life, do we inject religious belief into this debate? The answer is emphatically no. Even the NIH Human Embryo Research Panel, which recommended federal funding for destructive human embryo experiments, called the early human embryo "a developing form of human life" which "warrants serious moral consideration."[5] If some wish to deny membership in the human family to human beings in the earliest stage of their development, it is they who impose an ideological filter on the facts.[6] To claim that one is banning "human cloning" by simply banning the nurture or live birth of human embryos already produced by cloning is to distort language and common sense.

The church is also sensitive to claims that cloning is necessary for the pursuit of valuable medical research. We hold that "medicine is an eminent, essential form of service to mankind."[7] Research involving the cloning of animals, plants and even human genes, cells and tissues can be beneficial to human beings and presents no intrinsic moral problem. However, when research turns its attention to human subjects, we must be sure that we do not undermine human dignity in the very process of seeking to serve it. Human experimentation divorced from moral considerations may well progress more quickly on a technical level—but at the loss—of our sense of humanity. The Tuskegee syphilis study, Nazi Germany's hypothermia experiments and our own government's Cold War radiation experiments will always be remembered in the history of modern medicine—but not in a positive light. Any "progress" they may have brought on a technical level is far overshadowed by their mistreatment of human beings.

Ethical research alternatives

There has been much speculation in recent months about the ways human cloning might revolutionize medical research on various diseases. In all these areas of research, however, alternatives seem to be possible which do not involve the use of cloning technology to create and destroy human embryos. For example, some researchers may want to use somatic-cell nuclear transfer to create "customized stem-cell lines" genetically matched for individual patients—a procedure that in each case would require creating, developing and then killing a human embryo that is the patient's identical twin. Yet even the National Bioethics Advisory Commission described this avenue of research as "a rather expensive and far-fetched scenario," and reminded us that a moral assessment is necessary as well:

"Because of ethical and moral concerns raised by the use of embryos for research purposes, it would be far more desirable to explore the direct use of human cells of adult origin to produce specialized cells or tissues for transplantation into patients."[8]

Surely, anyone who understands the need for ethically responsible science can agree with this judgment. One great benefit of a ban on human cloning is that it will direct the scientific enterprise toward research that benefits human beings without forcing them to produce, exploit and destroy fellow human beings to gain those benefits. Creating human life solely to cannibalize and destroy it is the most unconscionable use of human cloning—not its highest justification.

Thank you for your attention. I would be glad to try to answer any questions.

Notes

1. Pontifical Academy of Life, "Human Cloning Is Immoral" (July 9, 1997), in The Pope Speaks, 43:I (January/February 1998), p. 29. Also see: Congregation for the Doctrine of the Faith, *Donum Vitae* (1987 Instruction on Respect for Human Life in its Origin and on the Dignity of Procreation), I.6 and II.B.

2. Leon R. Kass, "The Wisdom of Repugnance," in *The New Republic,* June 2, 1997, p. 23.

3. Examples include S. 1602 and S. 1611 now pending in the Senate. [Editor's Note: Both pieces of legislation failed to pass.]

4. Editorial, "Embryos: Drawing the Line," *The Washington Post,* Oct. 2, 1994, C6.

5. Final Report of the Human Embryo Research Panel (National Institutes of Health: Sept. 27, 1994), p. 2. Tragically, the panel gave no real weight to this insight in its final policy recommendations.

6. While some fertility specialists have used the term *pre-embryo* to describe the first 14 days of human development, a scientific expert who strongly supports embryo research recently wrote that this term was embraced "for reasons that are political, not scientific." The term *pre-embryo,* he writes, "is useful in the political arena—where decisions are made about whether to allow early embryo (now called pre-embryo) experimentation." Biologically, in the human species and others, an embryo exists from the one-celled stage onward. See Lee Silver, *Remaking Eden: Cloning and Beyond in a Brave New World* (Avon Books 1997), p. 39.

7. Pope John Paul II, address to the World Medical Association (Oct. 29, 1983); printed as "The Ethics of Genetic Manipulation," *Origins*, 13:23 (Nov. 17, 1983), p. 385.

8. *Cloning Human Beings: Report and Recommendations of the National Bioethics Advisory Commission* (Rockville, Md.: June 1997), pp. 30–31. The commission here outlined three alternative avenues of stem cell research, two of which seem not to involve creating human embryos at all.

9

The Cloning Debate
Redraws Political Alliances

William Saletan

William Saletan is a senior writer for Slate, *an online publication, and a contributing writer to* Mother Jones.

In the debates over human cloning and embryo research, many abortion opponents have reflexively opposed cloning research, while pro-choice activists have supported it. However, a closer examination of cloning reveals that both sides may find themselves in awkward positions when applying the reasoning behind their respective abortion positions to cloning.

Earlier this year [1998], when the Senate debated his bill to ban human cloning, Sen. Kit Bond (R-Mo.) was given 20 seconds to summarize the issue. "Science has given us partial-birth abortions and Dr. Kevorkian's assisted suicide," he declared. "We should say no to these scientific advances and no to the cloning of human embryos."

The next day, a bioethicist testified at a House committee meeting that cloned zygotes—egg cells activated by a DNA transplant from body cells—were human beings. "Do you believe that a woman should have a right to an abortion?" asked pro-choice Rep. Greg Ganske (R-Iowa). "I am very proudly pro-life," the witness snapped back.

It's not surprising that politicians and activists are treating the cloning debate as the next round of the abortion war. Few of them have a clue about the mechanics of cloning, much less the ethics. But they know their positions on abortion—pro-life or pro-choice—and their first instinct is to apply the same arguments to cloning. They don't yet understand how treacherous the new terrain is.

Pro-life quandaries

Pro-lifers are obsessed with legislation sponsored by Sens. Ted Kennedy (D-Mass.) and Dianne Feinstein (D-Calif.) that would permit the production of human zygotes through cloning but would ban their implantation in a womb. The National Right to Life Committee (NRLC), which takes no position on cloning per se, lobbied senators to reject the bill, saying that it would require researchers to "kill the embryos." The principle at stake, according to the Christian Coalition, is "the sanctity of each human life from conception until natural death."

But in cloning, there is no conception. The criteria by which pro-lifers define a new person—fusion of egg and sperm, a unique combination of genes—are never met. Applying these criteria, pro-life Sen. Orrin Hatch (R-Utah) calls cloned zygotes "asexually produced totipotent cells" and questions whether they are really embryos. That implies that fully born clones aren't people, a position the NRLC rejects. But to escape that nightmare, pro-lifers will have to rethink their definition of when life begins.

Pro-lifers also reject the assertion of human freedom over nature. In the abortion context, this is an argument for life. But in cloning, it becomes an argument against it. Cloning a human "for the purpose of bringing new life into the world is intrinsically evil and should be absolutely prohibited," declared Sen. Sam Brownback (R-Kan.) in support of the Bond bill. Sen. Jesse Helms (R-N.C.) agreed: "We should not be in the business of taking away life or creating life unnaturally." One of the "unnatural" practices forbidden by the Bond bill is the transfer of a nucleus from a fertilized but fragile egg to an enucleated healthy egg. This technique enables a woman to give birth to a child conceived by the fusion of egg and sperm, rather than suffer a spontaneous abortion. Yet pro-life senators supported legislation to ban it.

In the abortion debate, pro-lifers treat procreation and sexual responsibility as twin values: You had sex and got pregnant, so you should carry the child to term. But in cloning, the twin values come apart. The cloned zygote originates in a test tube, not a womb. So when NRLC legislative director Douglas Johnson says that embryos must not be "allowed to die without being implanted in a womb," it's not clear whose womb he has in mind. Foreseeing this dilemma, pro-lifers condemn asexual reproduction as a moral offense. In other words, if you want a baby, they insist that you have sex.

Pro-lifers further protest that cloned babies might be deformed. Bond told his colleagues that creating babies with "abnormalities" was "entirely unacceptable." Even if the child were physically normal, other pro-lifers objected, its family structure would be ruined by the nature of its creation. "Every child has a right not to be so born," a pro-life theologian told the House committee. Pro-lifers used to stand for equality, rejecting the view that children with physical disabilities or unfortunate origins (i.e., rape or incest) should never be born. Now they are embracing that view.

Pro-choice quandaries

Pro-choicers, too, are in danger of wandering astray. Two months before the Senate cloning debate, pro-choice legal scholar Laurence Tribe, writing in the *New York Times*, renounced the anti-cloning movement as an assault on "unconventional ways of linking erotic attachment, romantic commitment, genetic replication, gestational mothering, and the joys and responsibilities of child rearing."

In the Senate, Feinstein submitted a letter from the libertarian Cato

Institute suggesting that cloning could eventually be accepted as a solution to infertility. She urged her colleagues to heed a plea from the nation's leading advocacy group for infertile couples, which demanded: "Avenues for further research to help couples must not be halted." She also submitted a letter from the biotech company Genentech, which cautioned would-be cloning regulators not to tamper with "the legal rights of persons to free expression and inquiry in the private market."

As cloning grows from an embryonic curiosity to a mature political issue, advocates of choice and of life are increasingly finding themselves in . . . awkward positions.

In the abortion debate, the "choice" argument is anchored by the obligation to defend a woman's bodily integrity. But in cloning, she needs no such defense, because she isn't pregnant yet. Absent that anchor, the ideology of an unbounded right to replicate oneself in an "unconventional" arrangement of procreation, eroticism, and commitment—or lack of commitment—leads to chaos. Some pro-choicers pretend that cloning is just a small step from gay parenthood and in vitro fertilization, but it's not. Cloning abolishes the genetic difference between parent and child. If gay parenthood means that Heather has two mommies, cloning doesn't just mean that Heather has one mommy; it means that, genetically, Heather is her mommy. So if Heather's mommy has a husband and daughter, then genetically, Heather is her sister's mommy and her daddy's wife.

The argument becomes even more pernicious when coupled with the view, advanced by some abortion rights advocates, that bodily integrity is a property right. "Every person's DNA is his or her personal property," Randolfe Wicker of the Clone Rights United Front told the House committee. "To have that DNA cloned into another extended life is part and parcel of his or her right to control his or her own reproduction." If that's true, then you own your clone. And if you and your spouse conceive a child normally, don't you collectively own that child?

Furthermore, if DNA is property, it can be sold. In abortion, this is moot, because the embryo dies. But in cloning, it lives. Who will end up owning the clone and its DNA? With that in mind, you'd expect progressives to be wary of entrusting cloning to private interests. You'd think that Ted Kennedy, the scourge of greedy health insurance companies, would be last to deflect questions about the commercial cloning schemes of "our great research pharmaceutical companies" by equating their interests with those of the American Cancer Society and the American Heart Association. Yet there stood Kennedy at the climax of the Senate debate, boasting: "If they are special interest groups, we are proud to stand with them."

As cloning grows from an embryonic curiosity to a mature political issue, advocates of choice and of life are increasingly finding themselves in such awkward positions. They ought to ask how they got there and where they're going.

10

Religion Offers Guidance on Human Cloning

National Bioethics Advisory Commission

The National Bioethics Advisory Commission (NBAC) was established in 1995 to provide expert counsel to the president of the United States on bioethics issues. The panel was assigned to review and report on the ethical implications of human cloning in 1997. NBAC solicited testimony and information from religious leaders and theologians for the report's section on religious views on cloning.

Religious thinkers have been debating the morality of cloning for decades. A survey of theologians and religious leaders reveals a diverse spectrum of opinion on whether humans should be cloned. For some, religious beliefs provide a clear warning that cloning violates human dignity and is a form of "playing God." Others contend that more reflection is needed to determine whether cloning may be ethically acceptable in some cases.

It is possible to identify four recent overlapping periods in which theologians and other religious thinkers have considered the scientific prospects and ethics of the cloning of humans. The first phase, which began in the mid-1960s and continued into the early 1970s, was shaped by a context of expanded choices and control of reproduction (e.g., the availability of the birth control pill), the prospects of alternative, technologically-assisted reproduction (e.g., *in vitro* fertilization [IVF]), and the advocacy by some biologists and geneticists of cloning "preferred" genotypes, which, in their view, would avoid overloading the human gene pool with genes that are linked to deleterious outcomes and that could place the survival of the human species at risk.

Several prominent theologians engaged in these initial discussions of human genetic manipulation and cloning, including Charles Curran, Bernard Häring, Richard McCormick, and Karl Rahner within Roman Catholicism, and Joseph Fletcher and Paul Ramsey within Protestantism. The diametrically opposed positions staked out by the last two theologians gave an early signal of the wide range of views that

Excerpted from Chapter 3 of *Cloning Human Beings: Report and Recommendations of the National Bioethics Advisory Commission,* by the National Bioethics Advisory Commission, June 1997.

are still expressed by religious thinkers.

Joseph Fletcher advocated expansion of human freedom and control over human reproduction. He portrayed the cloning of humans as one of many present and prospective reproductive options that could be ethically justified by societal benefit. Indeed, for Fletcher, as a method of reproduction, cloning was preferable to the "genetic roulette" of sexual reproduction. He viewed laboratory reproduction as "radically human" because it is deliberate, designed, chosen, and willed (Fletcher, 1971, 1972, 1974, 1979).

By contrast, Paul Ramsey portrayed the cloning of humans as a "borderline" or moral boundary that could be crossed only at risk of compromise to humanity and to basic concepts of human procreation. Cloning threatened three "horizontal" (person-person) and two "vertical" (person-God) border crossings. First, clonal reproduction would require directed or managed breeding to serve the scientific ends of a controlled gene pool. Second, it would involve nontherapeutic experimentation on the unborn. Third, it would assault the meaning of parenthood by transforming "procreation" into "reproduction" and by severing the unitive end (expressing and sustaining mutual love) and the procreative end of human sexual expression. Fourth, the cloning of humans would express the sin of pride or hubris. Fifth, it could also be considered a sin of self-creation as humans aspire to become a "man-God" (Ramsey, 1966, 1970).

The values *that underlie religious concerns about cloning humans have endured and continue to inform public debate.*

A second era of theological reflection on cloning humans began in 1978, a year that was notable for two events, the birth in Britain of the first IVF baby, Louise Brown, and the publication of David Rorvik's *In His Image,* an account alleging (falsely) the creation of the first cloned human being (Rorvik, 1978).

This period also witnessed the beginning of formal ecclesiastical involvement with questions of genetic manipulation. In 1977 the United Church of Christ produced a study booklet on *Genetic Manipulation,* which appears to be the earliest reference to human cloning among Protestant denominational literature (Lynn, 1977). It provided a general overview of the science and ethics of cloning humans but stopped short of a specific theological verdict.

The discussions of the 1970s continued into the 1980s with particular attention to IVF, artificial insemination by donor, and surrogacy. These techniques challenged traditional notions of the family by separating genetic and rearing fatherhood and genetic, gestational, and rearing motherhood, as well as raising questions about whether the contractual and commercial ties in many of these arrangements were inimical to traditional religious views of the family.

A third era of religious discussion began in 1993 with the report from George Washington University of the separation of cells in human blastomeres to create multiple, genetically identical embryos. The Roman

Catholic Church expressed vigorous opposition to the procedure, and a Vatican editorial denounced the research as "intrinsically perverse." Catholic moral theologians invoked norms of individuality, dignity, and wholeness in condemning this research (McCormick, 1993, 1994). While many Conservative Protestant scholars held that this research contravened basic notions of personhood such as freedom, the sanctity of life, and the image of God, some other Protestant scholars noted its potential medical benefits and advocated careful regulation rather than prohibition.

The fourth and most recent stage of religious discussion has come in the wake of the successful cloning of Dolly the sheep through the somatic cell nuclear transfer technique, as the cloning of a human once again appeared to be a near-term possibility. Several Roman Catholic and Protestant thinkers have reiterated and reinforced past opposition and warnings.

However, some Protestant thinkers, in reflecting on the meaning of human partnership with ongoing divine creative activity, have expressed qualified support for cloning research and for creating children using somatic cell nuclear transfer techniques. Likewise, some Jewish and Islamic thinkers encourage continuing laboratory research on animal models and even laboratory work on the possibility of cloning human beings (only in pursuit of a worthy objective), while expressing deep moral reservations, at least at this time, about the transfer of a human embryo obtained by nuclear transfer techniques to a womb for purposes of gestation and birth.

Several conclusions emerge from this brief historical overview:

- Over the past twenty-five years, theologians have engaged in repeated discussions of the prospect of cloning humans that anticipate and illuminate much current religious discussion of this topic.
- Theological and ecclesiastical positions on cloning humans are pluralistic in their premises, their modes of argument, and even their conclusions. In short, they exhibit the pluralism characteristic of American religiosity.
- The religious discussion of cloning humans has connected it closely with ongoing debates about technologically assisted reproduction and genetic interventions.
- Despite changes in scientific research and technical capability, the *values* that underlie religious concerns about cloning humans have endured and continue to inform public debate.

Responsible human dominion over nature

Warnings Not To Play God. As often happens when a powerful new scientific tool is developed, the announcement that mammalian somatic cell nuclear transfer cloning was possible generated strong warnings against "playing God." This slogan is usually invoked as a moral stop sign to some scientific research or medical practice on the basis of one or more of the following distinctions between human beings and God:

- Human beings should not probe the fundamental secrets or mysteries of life, which belong to God.
- Human beings lack the authority to make certain decisions about the beginning or ending of life. Such decisions are reserved to divine sovereignty.
- Human beings are fallible and also tend to evaluate actions ac-

cording to their narrow, partial, and frequently self-interested perspectives.

- Human beings do not have the knowledge, especially knowledge of outcomes of actions, attributed to divine omniscience.
- Human beings do not have the power to control the outcomes of actions or processes that is a mark of divine omnipotence.

Even within religious communities, however, the warning against "playing God" may not be considered a sufficient argument against human cloning. Allen Verhey contends that this warning is simply too indiscriminate to provide ethical guidance. Furthermore, it overlooks moral invitations to play God, particularly in the realm of genetics (Verhey, 1995). While agreeing with Ramsey that human beings are not called to "play God," Protestant Ted Peters argues that this does not by itself define what is necessary for us to be human. Hence, we are responsible for using our creativity and freedom (features of the image of God) to forge a destiny more consonant with human dignity. In "playing human," Peters contends, there is not theological reason to leave human nature unchanged, and no theological principles that the cloning of humans necessarily violates (Peters, 1997).

Human dignity

Appeals to human dignity are prominent in Roman Catholic analyses and assessments of the prospects of human cloning, which base "human dignity" on the creation story and on the Christian account of God's redemption of human beings. The Catholic moral tradition views the cloning of a human being as "a violation of human dignity" (Haas, letter from the Pope John Center, 1997).

Religious thinkers generally do not question whether a person created through cloning is a human being created in God's image. They extend to persons created through cloning the same moral protections that already apply to other persons created in the image of God. For instance, Rabbi Elliot Dorff argues that "[n]o clone may . . . legitimately be denied any of the rights and protections extended to any other child" (Dorff, 1997, p. 5). However, many fear that the human dignity of persons created through cloning will be violated by the denial of such rights and protections, for instance, through enslavement to others and other forms of "man's mastery over man" (Tendler, 1997).

Human cloning would violate human dignity, according to some religious opponents, because it would "jeopardize the personal and unique identity of the clone (or clones) as well as the person whose genome was thus duplicated" (Haas, 1997). This problem does not arise in the case of identical twins, because neither is the "source or maker of the other" (Haas, 1997). Religious concerns about identity and individuality focus mainly on how persons created through cloning will inevitably or possibly be treated, rather than whether such persons are actually unique creatures in God's image. Rejecting genetic determinism, religious thinkers hold that cloning humans would "produce independent human beings with histories and influences all their own and with their own free will" (Dorff, 1997, p. 6). The person created through cloning will be "a new person, an integrated body and mind, with unique experiences." However, it will doubtless be harder for such persons "to establish their own identity and for their creators to acknowledge and respect it." (Dorff, 1997, p. 6). Even for absolute opponents, the process of cloning humans only *violates* human dignity; it does not *diminish* human dignity: "In the cloning of humans there is an affront to human dignity. . . . Yet, in no way is the human dignity of that person [the one who results from cloning] diminished" (Haas, 1997, p. 3).

Sanctity of life is one norm associated with human dignity. For instance, the prohibition of the shedding of human blood is connected with God's creation of humans in his own image (Genesis 9:6). Opponents often view the cloning of a human as a breach, or at least as a potential breach, of the sanctity of life. In rejecting human cloning, Joseph Cardinal Ratizinger of the Vatican insisted that "the sanctity of [human] life is untouchable" (quoted in Haas, 1997, p. 2). Even those who offer limited support for human cloning, in part on the grounds that it could be used in support of life, argue that it is necessary to set conditions and limits in order to prevent harm to persons who are created through cloning. Not only do they rule out such egregious violations of the sanctity of life as sacrificing persons created through cloning in order to obtain their organs for transplantation, they also worry about what will be done with the "bad results," that is, the "mistakes" that will be inevitable at least in the short term (Dorff, 1997, pp. 3-4). In addition, most recognize that the risks to persons created through cloning are now so unknown that we should virtually rule out human cloning for the present, because those who create children in this manner could not be sure that they are "doing no evil" (Tendler, 1997).

Even within religious communities, . . . the warning against "playing God" may not be considered a sufficient argument against human cloning.

Objectification also represents a fundamental breach of human dignity. To treat persons who are the sources of genetic material for cloning or persons who are created through cloning as mere objects, means, or instruments violates the religious principle of human dignity as well as the secular principle of respect for persons. Cloning humans would necessarily involve objectification, some religious thinkers argue, because it would treat the child as "an object of manipulation" by potentially eliminating the marital act and by attempting "to design and control the very identity of the child" (Haas, 1997). Cloning humans is wrong, in short, because "it subjects human individuals at their most vulnerable, at their very coming-into-being, to the arbitrary whim, power and manipulation of others" (Haas, 1997). For other religious thinkers who accept human cloning under some circumstances, it is necessary to reduce the effects of objectification, for example by a commitment to accept and care for the "mistakes" made in cloning (Dorff, 1997).

Objectification can become commodification when commercial and economic forces determine whether and how a person is treated as an object. Religious opponents of human cloning stress that objectification through commodification is a major risk and worry that "economic incentives will control when humans will be cloned" (Cahill, 1997, p. 3). Commodification would deny "the sacred character of human life depicted in the Jewish tradition, transforming it instead to fungible commodities on the human marketplace to be judged by a given person's worth to others" (Dorff, 1997, p. 2).

Procreation and families

Procreation and Reproduction. In the initial phase of theological debate about cloning humans, Paul Ramsey argued that the covenant of marriage includes the goods of sexual love and procreation, which are divinely ordained and intrinsically related: Human beings have no authority to sever what God had joined together. On this basis, Ramsey, a Protestant, joined with several Roman Catholic moral theologians, such as Bernard Häring and Richard McCormick, in objecting to the cloning of humans as part of the panoply of reproductive technologies. They claimed that such technologies separate the unitive and procreative ends of human sexuality and transform "procreation," which at most puts humans in a role of co-creator, into "reproduction." The Vatican's 1987 *Instruction on Respect for Human Life (Donum Vitae)* rejected human cloning either as a scientific outcome or technical proposal: "Attempts or hypotheses for obtaining a human being without any connection with sexuality through 'twin fission,' cloning, or parthenogenesis are to be considered contrary to the moral law, since they are in opposition to the dignity both of human procreation and the conjugal union" (Congregation for the Doctrine of the Faith, 1987).

Religious traditions usually approach the cloning of humans to create children from the standpoint of familial relationships . . . rather than . . . personal rights.

A similar critique distinguishes "begetting" (procreating) from "making" (reproducing). According to the Nicene Creed of early Christianity, Jesus, as the authentic image of God and the normative exemplar of personhood, is "begotten, not made" of God. The theological interpretation of "begetting" emphasizes likeness, identity, equality; begetting expresses the parent's very being. By contrast, "making" refers to unlikeness, alienation, and subordination; it expresses the parent's will as a project.

However, many religious thinkers do not accept the sharp separation between begetting and making, because it could rule out various reproductive technologies that they find acceptable, just as many do not accept the absolute connection between unitive and procreative meanings of sexual acts, in part because it would rule out artificial contraception, which they find acceptable. They may, nevertheless, still reject the cloning of humans to create children because they perceive it to be radically different from all other methods of technologically-assisted reproduction. Thus, they may stress the radically new features of human cloning, perhaps even viewing it as a "genuine revolution" in reproduction.

Concerns About the Family. Religious traditions usually approach the cloning of humans to create children from the standpoint of familial relationships and responsibilities rather than from the standpoint of personal rights and individual autonomy. Hence, a primary moral criterion is the impact of cloning humans on the integrity of the family, a concern that includes but also goes beyond the inseparable goods of marriage and the primacy of begetting over making.

Lisa Cahill, a Roman Catholic moral theologian, argues that "the child who is truly the child of a single parent is a genuine revolution in human history, and his or her advent should be viewed with immense caution." She further contends that cloning violates "the essential reality of human family and . . . the nature of the socially related individual within it. We all take part of our identity, both material or biological and social, from combined ancestral kinship networks. The existing practice of 'donating' gametes when the donors have no intention to parent the resulting child is already an affront to this order of things. But, in such cases, as in cases of adoption where the rearing of a child within its original combined-family network is impossible or undesirable, the child can still in fact claim the dual-lineage origin that characterizes every other human being. Whether socially recognized or not, this kind of ancestry is an important part of the human sense of self (as witnessed by searches for 'biological' parents and families), as well as a foundation of important human relationships." Cloning humans to create children, Cahill concludes, would constitute an "unprecedented rupture in those biological dimensions of embodied humanity which have been most important for social cooperation" (Cahill, testimony, 1997). At the extreme, cloning humans would not only free human reproduction from marital and male-female relationships, but would "allow for the emancipation of human reproduction from *any* relationship" (Mohler, 1997).

Concerns about lineage and intergenerational relations in other religious traditions also set limits on or challenge the cloning of humans to create children. For example, Islamic scholar Abdulaziz Sachedina suggests that Islam could accept some therapeutic uses of human cloning "as long as the lineage of the child remains religiously unblemished" (Sachedina, 1997, pp. 6–7). And some Jewish thinkers worry that cloning humans may diminish the ethic of responsibility because of changed roles (father, mother, child) and relationships (spousal, parental, filial).

Assessments of acts and public policies

Religious perspectives on public policies regarding human cloning vary for several reasons. One critical factor is whether the tradition views every possible act of cloning humans as intrinsically evil (as, for example, Roman Catholicism does) or whether it recognizes that cloning humans could conceivably be justified in some circumstances, however few they may be (as, for example, many in the Jewish tradition do). The Roman Catholic tradition argues that the very *use* of cloning techniques to create human beings is contrary to human dignity: "One may not use, even for a single instance, a means for achieving a good purpose which intrinsically is morally flawed" (Haas, 1997, p. 4). And, for that tradition, creating a child through human cloning is intrinsically morally flawed. Some thinkers in other traditions also hold that such an action is always morally wrong, whatever good might come from it. (see Meilaender, 1997).

By contrast, some other religious thinkers believe that cloning a human to create a child could be religiously and morally acceptable under certain conditions. They may view the technology as "morally neutral" (Dorff, 1997) and then consider which uses are morally justified; or they may oppose human cloning from matured (differentiated) cells except in the most exceptional circumstances and then identify those exceptional circumstances.

The Roman Catholic tradition argues that the very use of cloning techniques to create human beings is contrary to human dignity.

Two hypothetical scenarios are quite common. The first one involves cloning a sterile person to create a child. Rabbi Tendler poses the case of "a young man who is sterile, whose family was wiped out in the Holocaust, and [who] is the last of a genetic line." Rabbi Tendler says "I would certainly clone him" (Tendler, 1997, transcript, p. 35). The debate about this type of case hinges in part on different views of infertility. The Jewish tradition often views infertility as an "illness" and thus brings it under the responsibility to heal. According to others, for example, some in the Protestant tradition, the problem of infertility is not serious enough to warrant research into or actual human cloning (see Duff, 1997, p. 5).

A second case involves cloning a person who has a serious and perhaps fatal disease and needs a compatible source of biological material, such as bone marrow. Rabbi Dorff, for instance, holds that it would be "legitimate from a moral and a Jewish point of view" to clone a person with leukemia with the intent of transplanting bone marrow from the created child as long as the "parents" intend to raise the child as they would raise any other child (Dorff, 1997, pp. 4-5; see also Tendler, 1997). Some Protestants concur on this case, even when they reject the first type of case (see Duff, 1997, p. 4). Those who consider the second type of case justifiable rule out destruction or abandonment of the created child, as well as the imposition of serious risks of harm. Indeed, acceptance of either type of hypothetical case—as well as a third type of case involving the cloning of a dying child—presupposes that the procedure is safe for the child created by cloning. Other conditions include the protection of the created child's rights and the lack of acceptable alternatives to cloning persons in such cases.

Those who view cloning humans as intrinsically wrong may also respond sympathetically and compassionately to people's suffering when they are infertile or have a disease that brings death or disability. However, they usually hold that the good of overcoming this suffering does not justify cloning humans: Cloning "is entirely unsuitable for human procreation even for exceptional circumstances"(Haas, 1997, p. 4). Indeed, religious critics may view the exceptional circumstances featured in the cases as "temptations" to be resisted (see Meilaender, 1997, p. 5).

Some rough correlations hold between evaluations of particular cases and proposals for public policy. Religious thinkers who view the cloning of a human being as intrinsically wrong, i.e., wrong in and of itself, under any and all circumstances, tend to support a permanent ban on cloning humans through legislative and other means. Any use of cloning technology to create a human child abuses that technology, which is, however, acceptable in animal reproduction. By contrast, religious thinkers who hold that, in some conceivable circumstances, it could be morally justifiable to clone a person to create a child tend to support public policies that regulate the procedure, with varying restrictions, or that ban the procedure for the time being or until certain conditions are met. In assessing public policies, this second group is particularly concerned to prevent potential abuses of the technology in cloning humans rather than condemning all uses.

Most religious thinkers who recommend public policies on cloning humans propose either a ban or restrictive regulation. A few examples will suffice. On March 6, 1997, the Christian Life Commission of the Southern Baptist Convention issued a resolution entitled "Against Human Cloning," which supported President Clinton's decision to prohibit federal funding for human-cloning research and requested "that the Congress of the United States make human cloning unlawful." The resolution also called on "all nations of the world to make efforts to prevent the cloning of any human being."

There is no single "religious" view on cloning humans.

The Vatican's 1987 *Instruction on Respect for Human Life (Donum Vitae)* argued for a legal prohibition of human cloning, as well as many other reproductive technologies. Official Roman Catholic statements since that time have condemned nontherapeutic research on human embryos and human cloning and have called on governments around the world to enact prohibitive legislation. Most recently, in the wake of the cloning of Dolly, a Vatican statement reiterated the basic teaching of *Donum Vitae*: "A person has the right to be born in a human way. It is to be strongly hoped that states . . . will immediately pass a law that bans the application of cloning of humans and that in the face of pressures, they have the force to make no concessions."

By contrast, Rabbi Elliot Dorff argues that "human cloning should be regulated, not banned." He holds that "the Jewish demand that we do our best to provide healing makes it important that we take advantage of the promise of cloning to aid us in finding cures for a variety of diseases and in overcoming infertility." However, "the dangers of cloning . . . require that it be supervised and restricted." More specifically, "cloning should be allowed only for medical research or therapy; the full and equal status of clones with other fetuses or human beings must be recognized, with the equivalent protections guarded; and careful policies must be devised to determine how cloning mistakes will be identified and handled" (Dorff, 1997). Although Dorff stresses legislation, particularly to regulate privately funded research, he recognizes that legislation will be only partially effective, and for that reason calls for increased attention to hospital ethics committees and institutional review boards, in part because of the self-regulation involved. Hence, although legislation is important "to ban the most egregious practices," most supervision "should come from self-regulation akin to what we already have in place for experiments on human subjects" (Dorff, 1997, p. 15).

No single view on cloning

The wide variety of religious traditions and beliefs epitomizes the pluralism of American culture. Moreover, religious perspectives on cloning humans differ in fundamental premises, modes of reasoning, and conclusions. As a result, there is no single "religious" view on cloning humans, any more than for most moral issues in biomedicine. Nevertheless, discourse on many contested issues in biomedicine still proceeds across religious traditions, as well as secular traditions. Specifically with regard to cloning humans to create children, some religious thinkers believe that this technology could have some legitimate uses and thus could be justified under some circumstances if perfected; however, they may argue for regulation because of the danger of abuses or even for a ban, perhaps temporary, in light of concerns about safety. Other religious thinkers deny that this technology has any legitimate uses, contending that it always violates fundamental moral norms, such as human dignity. Such thinkers often argue for a legislative ban on all cloning of humans to create children. Finally, religious communities and thinkers draw on ancient and diverse traditions of moral reflection to address the cloning of humans, a subject they have debated off and on over the last thirty years. For some, fundamental religious beliefs and norms provide a clear negative answer: It is now and will continue to be wrong to clone a human. Others, however, hold that more reflection is needed, given new scientific and technological developments, to determine exactly how to interpret and evaluate the prospect of human cloning in light of fundamental religious convictions and norms.

References

Cahill, L.S., "Cloning: Religion-Based Perspectives," Testimony before the National Bioethics Advisory Commission, March 13, 1997.

Congregation for the Doctrine of the Faith, *Instruction on Respect for Human Life in Its Origin and on the Dignity of Procreation* (Rome, 1987).

Dorff, R.E.N., "Human Cloning: A Jewish Perspective," Testimony before the National Bioethics Commission, March 14, 1997.

Duff, N.J., "Theological Reflections on Human Cloning," Testimony presented to the National Bioethics Advisory Commission, March 13, 1997.

Fletcher, J., *Humanhood: Essays in Biomedical Ethics* (Buffalo, NY: Prometheus Books, 1979).

Fletcher, J., *The Ethics of Genetic Control* (Garden City, NY: Anchor Press, 1974).

Fletcher, J., "New Beginnings in Human Life: A Theologian's Response," *The New Genetics and the Future of Man*, M. Hamilton (ed.) (Grand Rapids, MI:

Wm. B. Eerdmans Publishing Company, 1972, 78, 79).

Fletcher, J., "Ethical Aspects of Genetics Controls," *New England Journal of Medicine* 285(14):776–783, 1971.

Haas, J.M., letter from the Pope John Center, submitted to the National Bioethics Advisory Commission, March 31, 1997.

Lynn, B., *Genetic Manipulation* (New York: Office for Church in Society, United Church of Christ, 1977).

McCormick, R.A., "Blastomere separation: Some concerns," *Hastings Center Report* 24 (2): 14-16, 1994.

McCormick, R.A., "Should we clone humans?" *The Christian Century* 17-24: 1148-1149, November 1993.

Meilaender, G.C., Testimony before the National Bioethics Advisory Commission, March 13, 1997.

Mohler, R.A., "The Brave New World of Cloning: A Christian Worldview Perspective," (unpublished manuscript, March 1997).

Peters, T., *Playing God? Genetic Discrimination and Human Freedom* (New York: Routledge, 1997).

Ramsey, P., "Moral and Religious Implications of Genetic Control," *Genetics and the Future of Man,* John D. Roslansky (ed.) (New York: Appleton-Century-Croffs, 1966).

Ramsey, P., *Fabricated Man: The Ethics of Genetic Control* (New Haven: Yale University Press, 1970).

Rorvik, D., *In His Image: The Cloning of a Man* (Philadelphia: J.B. Lippincott Company, 1978).

Sachedina, A., "Islamic Perspectives on Cloning," Testimony before the National Bioethics Advisory Commission, March 14, 1997.

Tendler, R.M., Testimony before the National Bioethics Advisory Commission, March 14, 1997.

Verhey, A., "Playing God and invoking a perspective," *Journal of Medicine and Philosophy* 20: 347-364, 1995.

This is an abridged version of chapter 3 of NBAC report on human cloning (June 1997). Much of the material in the original version is derived from a commissioned paper prepared for the National Bioethics Advisory Commission by Courtney S. Campbell, Department of Philosophy, Oregon State University, titled "Religious Perspectives on Human Cloning."

11

Religious Arguments Have No Place in the Debate over Human Cloning

Ronald A. Lindsay

Ronald A. Lindsay is a lawyer and philosopher.

The dogmatic pronouncements of religious leaders have little to offer in the continuing debate over human cloning. There is no necessary connection between religion and morality. The potential harms of cloning can be minimized through the rational application of secular ethical principles.

The furor following the announcement of recent experiments in cloning, including the cloning of the sheep Dolly, has prompted representatives of various religious groups to inform us of God's views on cloning. Thus, the Reverend Albert Moraczewski of the National Conference of Catholic Bishops has announced that cloning is "intrinsically morally wrong" as it is an attempt to "play God" and "exceed the limits of the delegated dominion given to the human race." Moreover, according to Reverend Moraczewski, cloning improperly robs people of their uniqueness. Dr. Abdulaziz Sachedina, an Islamic scholar at the University of Virginia, has declared that cloning would violate Islam's teachings about family heritage and eliminate the traditional role of fathers in creating children. Gilbert Meilaender, a Protestant scholar at Valparaiso University in Indiana, has stated that cloning is wrong because the point of the clone's existence "would be grounded in our will and desires" and cloning severs "the tie that united procreation with the sexual relations of a man and woman." On the other hand, Moshe Tendler, a professor of medical ethics at Yeshiva University, has concluded that there is religious authority for cloning, pointing out that respect for "sanctity of life would encourage us to use cloning if only for one individual . . . to prevent the loss of genetic line."

This is what we have come to expect from religious authorities: dog-

Reprinted from "Taboos Without a Clue: Sizing Up Religious Objections to Cloning," by Ronald A. Lindsay, *Free Inquiry,* Summer 1997. Reprinted with permission.

matic pronouncements without any support external to a particular religious tradition, self-justifying appeals to a sect's teachings, and metaphor masquerading as reasoned argument. And, of course, the interpreters of God's will invariably fail to agree among themselves as to precisely what actions God would approve.

Given that these authorities have so little to offer by way of impartial, rational counsel, it would seem remarkable if anyone paid any attention to them. However, not only do these authorities have an audience, but their advice is sought out by the media and government representatives. Indeed, President Clinton's National Bioethics Advisory Commission devoted an entire day to hearing testimony from various theologians.

Questionable ethics

The theologians' honored position reflects our culture's continuing conviction that there is a necessary connection between religion and morality. Most Americans receive instruction in morality, if at all, in the context of religious belief. As a result, they cannot imagine morality apart from religion, and when confronted by doubts about the morality of new developments in the sciences—such as cloning—they invariably turn to their sacred writings or to their religious leaders for guidance. Dr. Ebbie Smith, a professor at Southwestern Baptist Theological Seminary, spoke for many Americans when he insisted that the Bible was relevant to the cloning debate because "the Bible contains God's revelation about what we ought to be and do, if we can understand it."

But the attempt to extrapolate a coherent, rationally justifiable morality from religious dogma is a deeply misguided project. To begin, as a matter of logic, we must first determine what is moral before we decide what "God" is telling us. As Plato pointed out, we cannot deduce ethics from "divine" revelation until we first determine which of the many competing revelations are authentic. To do that, we must establish which revelations make moral sense. Morality is logically prior to religion.

> *Given the limits of the world of the Bible and the Koran, their authors simply had no occasion to address some of the problems that confront us, such as . . . cloning.*

Moreover, most religious traditions were developed millennia ago, in far different social and cultural circumstances. While some religious precepts retain their validity because they reflect perennial problems of the human condition (for example, no human community can maintain itself unless basic rules against murder and stealing are followed), others lack contemporary relevance. The world of the biblical patriarchs is not our world. Rules prohibiting the consumption of certain foods or prescribing limited, subordinate roles for women might have some justification in societies lacking proper hygiene or requiring physical strength for survival. But they no longer have any utility and persist only as irrational taboos. In addition, given the limits of the world of the Bible and the Koran, their authors simply had no occasion to address some of the problems that confront us, such as the ethics of *in vitro* fertilization, genetic engineering, or cloning. To pretend otherwise, and to try to apply religious precepts by extension and analogy to these novel problems is an act of pernicious self-delusion.

To underscore these points, let us consider some of the more common objections to cloning that have been voiced by various religious leaders:

Cloning is playing God. This is the most common religious objection, and its appearance in the cloning debate was preceded by its appearance in the debate over birth control, the debate over organ transplants, the debate over assisted dying, etc. Any attempt by human beings to control and shape their lives in ways not countenanced by some religious tradition will encounter the objection that we are "playing God." To say that the objection is uninformative is to be charitable. The objection tells us nothing and obscures much. It cannot distinguish between interferences with biological process that are commonly regarded as permissible (for example, use of analgesics or antibiotics) and those that remain controversial. Why is cloning an impermissible usurpation of God's authority, but not the use of tetracycline?

Cloning is unnatural because it separates reproduction from human sexual activity. This is the flip side of the familiar religious objection to birth control. Birth control is immoral because it severs sex from reproduction. Cloning is immoral because it severs reproduction from sex. One would think that allowing reproduction to occur without all that nasty, sweaty carnal activity might appeal to some religious authorities, but apparently not. In any event, the "natural" argument is no less question-begging in the context of reproduction without sex than it is in the context of sex without reproduction. "Natural" most often functions as an approbative and indefinable adjective; it is a superficially impressive way of saying, "This is good, I approve." Without some argument as to why something is "natural" and "good" or "unnatural" or "bad," all we have is noise.

Cloning robs persons of their God-given uniqueness and dignity. Why? Persons are more than the product of their genes. Persons also reflect their experiences and relationships. Furthermore, this argument actually demeans human beings. It implies that we are like paintings or prints: the more copies that are produced, the less each is worth. To the contrary, each clone will presumably be valued as much by their friends, lovers, and spouses as individuals who are produced and born in the traditional manner and not genetically duplicated.

Beyond theology

All the foregoing objections assume that cloning could successfully be applied to human beings. It is worth noting that this issue is not entirely free from doubt since Dolly was produced only after hundreds of attempts. And although in principle the same techniques should work in humans, biological experiments cannot always be repeated across different species.

Of course, if some of the religious have their way, the general public may never know whether cloning would work in humans, as research into applications of cloning to human beings could be outlawed or driven underground. This would be an unfortunate development. Quite apart from the obvious, arguably beneficial, uses of cloning, such as asexual reproduction for those incapable of having children through sex, there are potential spinoffs from cloning research that could prove extremely valuable. Doctors, for example, could develop techniques to take skin cells from someone with liver disease, reconfigure them to function as liver cells, clone them, and then transplant them back into the patient. Such a procedure would avoid the sometimes-fatal complications that accompany genetically nonidentical transplants as well as problems caused by the chronic shortage of available organs for transplant.

This is not to discount the potential for harm and abuse that would result from the development of cloning technology, especially if we also master techniques for manipulating DNA. If we are able to modify a human being's genetic composition to achieve a predetermined end and can then create clones from the modified genetic structure, we could, theoretically, create a humanlike order of animals that would be more intelligent than other animals but less intelligent and more docile than (other?) human beings. Sort of ready-made slaves.

But religious precepts are neither necessary nor sufficient for avoiding such dangers. What we require is a secular morality based on our needs and interests and the needs and interests of other sentient beings. In considering the example just given, it is apparent that harmful consequences to normal human beings could result from the creation of these humanoid slaves, as many could be deprived of a means of earning their livelihood. It would also lead to an enormous and dangerous concentration of power in the hands of those who controlled these humanoids. And, although in the abstract we cannot decide what rights these humanoids would have, it is probable that, as sentient beings with at least rudimentary intelligence, they would have a right to be protected from ruthless exploitation and, therefore, we could not morally permit them to be treated as slaves. Even domesticated animals have a right to be protected from cruel and capricious treatment.

Obviously, I have not listed all the factors that would have to be considered in evaluating the moral implications of my thought experiment. I have not even tried to list all the factors that would have to be considered in assessing the many other ways—some of them now unimaginable—in which cloning technology might be applied. My point here is that we have a capacity to address these moral problems as they arise in a rational and deliberate manner if we rely on secular ethical principles. The call by many of the religious for an absolute ban on cloning experiments is a tacit admission that their theological principles are not sufficiently powerful and adaptable to guide us through this challenging future.

I want to make clear that I am not saying we should turn a deaf ear to those who offer us moral advice on cloning merely because they are religious. Many bioethicists who happen to have deep religious convictions have made significant, valuable contributions to this field of moral inquiry. They have done so, however, by offering secular and objective grounds for their arguments. Just as an ethicist's religious background does not entitle her to a special deference, so too her religious background does not warrant her exclusion from the debate, provided she appeals to reason and not supernatural revelation.

Organizations to Contact

The editors have compiled the following list of organizations concerned with the issues debated in this book. The descriptions are derived from materials provided by the organizations. All have publications or information available for interested readers. The list was compiled on the date of publication of the present volume; names, addresses, and phone numbers may change. Be aware that many organizations take several weeks or longer to respond to inquiries, so allow as much time as possible.

American Life League (ALL)
PO Box 1350
Stafford, VA 22555
(888) 546-2580
website: www.all.org

ALL is an educational pro-life organization that opposes abortion, reproductive technologies, and fetal experimentation. It views human cloning and embryo research as immoral. Publications of the organization include the magazine *Celebrate Life*. It also publishes articles about cloning on its website.

Biotechnology Industry Organization (BIO)
1625 K St. NW, Suite 1100, Washington, DC 20006
(202) 857-0244
website: www.bio.org

The BIO represents biotechnology companies, academic institutions, state biotechnology centers, and related organizations that support the use of biotechnology in improving health care, agriculture, the environment, and other fields. It opposes the cloning of human beings, but also opposes sweeping legislative bans on human cloning on the grounds that such laws would unfairly restrict important biomedical research on human genes, tissues, and cells. The organization publishes the magazine *Your World, Our World*, and its statements on human cloning and federal regulation are available on its website.

Center for Bioethics and Human Dignity (CBHD)
2065 Half Day Rd., Bannockburn, IL 60015
(847) 317-8180 • fax: (847) 317-8153
website: www.bioethix.org

CBHD is an international education center whose purpose is to bring Christian perspectives to bear on contemporary bioethical challenges facing society. Its publications address genetic technologies as well as other topics such as euthanasia and abortion. It publishes the newsletter *Dignity* and the book *Genetic Ethics: Do the Ends Justify the Genes?*

Center for Bioethics at the University of Pennsylvania
3401 Market St., Suite 320, Philadelphia, PA 19104-3308
(215) 898-7136 • fax: (215) 573-3036
website: http://bioethics.net

The University of Pennsylvania's Center for Bioethics is the largest center of its kind in the world. It engages in research and publishes articles about many areas of bioethics, including cloning and genetic engineering. *PennBioethics* is its quarterly newsletter.

Federation of American Societies for Experimental Biology (FASEB)
Office of Public Affairs
9650 Rockville Pike, Bethesda, MD 20814-3998
(301) 571-7795
website: www.faseb.org

FASEB is the largest professional association of biologists in the United States. Its Office of Public Affairs monitors public developments affecting biomedical research and works to develop a consensus on public policy issues. In 1997, FASEB announced a five-year voluntary moratorium on attempts to clone humans. Its publications include *Cloning: Past, Present, and the Exciting Future.*

Food and Drug Adminstration (FDA)
200 C St. SW, Washington, DC 20204
(888) 463-6332
website: www.fda.gov

Part of the U.S. Department of Health and Human Services, the FDA is a public health agency charged with protecting American consumers from unsafe food and drugs. It oversees research in investigational new drugs (IND); and in 1998 it announced that it has regulatory authority over clinical research involving the cloning of human beings to ensure the safety of such experiments. The FDA publishes *FDA Consumer* magazine.

Foundation on Economic Trends (FET)
1660 L St. NW, Suite 216, Washington, DC 20036
(202) 466-2823 • fax: (202) 429-9602
website: www.biotechcentury.org

Founded by science critic and author Jeremy Rifkin, the foundation is a nonprofit organization whose mission is to examine emerging trends in science and technology and their impacts on the environment, the economy, culture, and society. FET works to educate the public about topics such as gene patenting, commercial eugenics, genetic discrimination, and cloning. Its website contains articles and news updates.

The Hastings Center
Route 9D, Garrison, NY 10524-5555
(914) 424-4040 • fax: (914) 424-4545
website: www.hastingscenter.org

The Hastings Center is an independent research institute that explores the medical, ethical, and social ramifications of biomedical advances. The center publishes books, papers, and the bimonthly *Hastings Center Report.*

Human Cloning Foundation
PMB 143, 1100 Hammond Dr., Suite 410A, Atlanta, GA 30328
website: www.humancloning.org

The foundation is a nonprofit organization that promotes education about human cloning and other forms of biotechnology and emphasizes the positive aspects of these technologies. Its website contains numerous articles and fact sheets on the benefits of human cloning.

Kennedy Institute of Ethics
Georgetown University
1437 37th St. NW, Washington, DC 20057
(202) 687-8099 • library: (800) 633-3849 • fax: (202) 687-6779
website: http://guweb.georgetown.edu/kennedy/

The institute sponsors research on medical ethics, including ethical issues surrounding human cloning. It supplies the National Library of Medicine with an online database on bioethics and publishes an annual bibliography in addition to reports and articles on specific issues concerning medical ethics.

National Bioethics Advisory Commission (NBAC)
6100 Executive Blvd., Suite 5B01, Rockville, MD 20592-7508
(301) 402-4242 • fax: (301) 480-6900
website: www.bioethics.gov

NBAC is a federal agency that sets ethical guidelines governing biomedical research. It works to protect the rights and welfare of human research subjects and governs the management and use of genetic information. Its published reports include *Cloning Human Beings* and *Ethical Issues in Human Stem Cell Research*.

National Institutes of Health (NIH)
1 Center Dr., Bdg. 1, Suite 126, Bethesda, MD 20892
(401) 496-2433
website: www.nih.gov

NIH is the federal government's primary agency for the support of biomedical research. It is the government agency responsible for developing guidelines for research on stem cells. It publishes information on its programs and activities on its website.

Bibliography

Books

Bryan Appleyard
Brave New Worlds: Staying Human in the Genetic Future. New York: Viking, 1998.

Bill Clinton
Cloning Prohibition Act of 1997: Message from the President of the United States. Washington, DC: Government Printing Office, 1997.

Ronald Cole-Turner, ed.
Human Cloning: Religious Responses. Louisville, KY: Westminster John Knox, 1997.

James C. Hefley and Lane P. Lester
Human Cloning: Playing God or Scientific Progress? Grand Rapids, MI: Fleming H. Ravell, 1998.

Leon R. Kass and James Q. Wilson
The Ethics of Human Cloning. Washington, DC: AEI, 1998.

Gina Kolata
Clone: The Road to Dolly and the Path Ahead. New York: William Morrow, 1998.

George J. Marlin
The Politician's Guide to Assisted Suicide, Cloning, and Other Current Controversies. Dulles, VA: Morley Institute, 1998.

Glenn McGee, ed.
The Human Cloning Debate. Berkeley, CA: Berkeley Hills, 1998.

National Bioethics Advisory Commission
Cloning Human Beings: Report and Recommendations of the National Bioethics Advisory Commission. Rockville, MD: NBAC, 1997.

Martha Nussbaum and Cass Sunstein, eds.
Clones and Clones: Facts and Fantasies About Human Cloning. New York: W.W. Norton, 1997.

Gregory E. Pence
Who's Afraid of Human Cloning? Lanham, MD: Rowman & Littlefield, 1998.

Gregory E. Pence, ed.
Flesh of My Flesh: The Ethics of Cloning Humans: A Reader. Lanham, MD: Rowman & Littlefield, 1998.

M.L. Rantala and Arthur J. Milgram, eds.
Cloning: For and Against. Chicago: Open Court, 1999.

Lee M. Silver
Remaking Eden: Cloning and Beyond in a Brave New World. New York: Avon, 1997.

Periodicals

Lori B. Andrews
"Mom, Dad, Clone: Implications for Reproductive Privacy," *Cambridge Quarterly of Healthcare Ethics*, Spring 1998.

Ronald Bailey — "The Twin Paradox: What Exactly Is Wrong with Cloning People?" *Reason*, May 1997.

Daniel Callahan — "Cloning: Then and Now," *Cambridge Quarterly of Healthcare Ethics*, Spring 1998.

Jonathan R. Cohen — "Cloning and Creation in Jewish Thought," *Hastings Center Report*, July/August 1999.

Commonweal — "Cloning Isn't Sexy," March 28, 1997.

Russell B. Connors Jr. — "The Ethics of Cloning," *St. Anthony Messenger*, March 1998.

Jennifer Couzin — "The Promise and Peril of Stem Cell Research," *U.S. News & World Report*, May 31, 1999.

CQ Researcher — "Embryo Research," December 17, 1999.

Dena S. Davis — "A Tale of Two Creatures: Jewish and Christian Attitudes Toward Cloning," *Park Ridge Center Bulletin*, March/April 1999.

Richard Dawkins — "Thinking Clearly About Clones," *Free Inquiry*, Summer 1997.

Gregg Easterbrook — "Medical Evolution: Will Homo Sapiens Become Obsolete?" *New Republic*, March 1, 1999.

Mark D. Eibert — "Clone Wars," *Reason*, June 1998.

Jean Bethke Elshtain — "Bad Seed," *New Republic*, February 9, 1998.

Ellen Wilson Fielding — "Fear of Cloning," *Human Life Review*, Spring 1997.

Kevin T. Fitzgerald — "Human Cloning: Analysis and Evaluation," *Cambridge Quarterly of Healthcare Ethics*, Spring 1998.

Sarah Franklin — "The Ethics of Human Cloning," *Society*, July/August 1999.

Tim Friend — "Getting to the Nucleus of Cloning Concerns," *USA Today*, March 12, 1997.

John Harris — "'Goodbye Dolly?' The Ethics of Human Cloning," *Journal of Medical Ethics*, December 1997.

Axel Kahn — "Clone Mammals . . . Clone Man," *Nature*, vol. 396, 1997.

Leon R. Kass — "The Wisdom of Repugnance: Why We Should Ban the Cloning of Humans," *New Republic*, June 2, 1997.

John F. Kilner — "Stop Cloning Around," *Christianity Today*, April 28, 1997.

R.C. Lewontin — "The Confusion over Cloning," *New York Review of Books*, October 23, 1997.

M. Therese Lysaught — "Pandora's Box," *Commonweal*, December 18, 1998.

Ruth Macklin — "Human Cloning? Don't Just Say No," *U.S. News & World Report*, March 10, 1997.

Robert G. McKinnell and Marie A. Di Berardino
"The Biology of Cloning: History and Rationale," *BioScience*, November 1999.

John J. Miller
"Hard Cell," *National Review*, April 5, 1999.

Virginia Morell
"A Clone of One's Own," *Discover*, May 1998.

J. Madeleine Nash
"The Case for Cloning," *Time*, February 9, 1998.

John O'Connor
"Human Cloning: Efficiency vs. Ethics," *Origins*, April 10, 1997.

Leslie Roberts
"How to Build a Better Bull: A New Style of Cloning," *U.S. News & World Report*, January 17, 2000.

Thomas A. Shannon
"Cloning Myths," *Commonweal*, April 10, 1998.

Lee M. Silver
"Cloning, Ethics, and Religion," *Cambridge Quarterly of Healthcare Ethics*, Spring 1998.

Peter Steinfels
"Cloning: Taking Ethics Seriously," *Responsive Community*, Spring 1997.

Lindsay Van Gelder
"Hello, Dolly, Hello, Dolly," *Ms.*, May/June 1997.

Ian Wilmut
"Dolly's False Legacy," *Time*, January 11, 1999.

Phil Wogaman
"Cloning: The Theological Implications," *Christian Social Action*, May 1997.

Index